Church and Family Together

Church and Family Together

A Congregational Manual for Black Family Ministry

Edited by Karen Jones Bernstine

Judson Press ® Valley Forge

Church and Family Together: A Congregational Manual for Black Family Ministry
© 1996 Judson Press, Valley Forge, PA 19482-0851

Bible quotations in this volume are from the NEW REVISED STANDARD VERSION of the Bible, copyrighted 1989 by the Division of Christian Education of the National Council of the Churches of Christ in the United States of America, and are used by permission. The Revised Standard Version of the Bible, copyright © 1946, 1952, 1971, by the Division of Christian Education of the National Council of Churches of Christ in the USA. Used by permission.

Library of Congress Cataloging-in-Publication Data

Church and family together : a congregational manual for Black family ministry / edited by Karen Jones Bernstine.
    p. cm.
    Includes bibliographical references.
    ISBN 0-8170-1243-5 (pbk. : alk. paper)
    1. Church work with Afro-American families. 2. Afro-Americans—Religion. I. Bernstine, Karen Jones.
BV4468.2.A34C48 1996
259'.1'08996073—dc20   95-47037

Printed in the U.S.A.

05 04 03 02 01 00 99 98 97 96

10 9 8 7 6 5 4 3 2 1

This manual was commissioned by the National Council of Churches of Christ Black Family Ministry Project.

Supporting Agencies

Lilly Endowment, Inc.
Children's Defense Fund
United Auto Workers

Participating Denominations

American Baptist Churches
African Methodist Episcopal Church
African Methodist Episcopal Zion Church
The Christian Church (Disciples of Christ)
Christian Methodist Episcopal Church
Evangelical Lutheran Church in America
The Moravian Church in America
National Baptist Convention, USA, Inc.
National Council of Churches of Christ
Presbyterian Church (U.S.A.)
United Church of Christ
United Methodist Church

Contributing Writers:

Karen Jones Bernstine
Louise Bates Evans
Marilyn Magee
Virginia Sargent

93526

The Purpose of this Manual

This congregational manual for family ministry in black congregations has been written to challenge the black church to reclaim its role as the basic social structure in supporting and advocating for black families. Throughout history the church has been a buffer against destructive forces that impinged upon black family life. The church has been the moral conscience of black people, a catalyst for their survival and success, a voice for social and political resistance, and a community called to live as family. On the threshold of the twenty-first century, congregations are still being called to live as the family of God, ministering throughout the community, leaving no one out, for as Jesus said, "Just as you did it to one of the least of these who are members of my family, you did it to me" (Matthew 25:40).

The need for such a manual was identified through the *Leadership Training Project for Family Ministry in Black Congregations.* It is the product of three years of intensive planning, training, site visits, evaluation, and follow-up. This manual shares the information that was learned throughout the project and builds upon those learnings. The manual is a resource/tool designed to be used either by a congregation working with a trained consultant or by a congregation working alone and utilizing its own resources.

The manual offers suggestions and ideas for planning, implementing, and/or strengthening ministry with black families. The writers affirm the diversity of families, communities, and congregations. We hope that you will use what you can and/or adapt any materials to your specific situation.

A list of commissioned consultants who are eager to assist you is included in Appendix B. The manual completes the *Leadership Training Project for Family Ministry in Black Congregations*. This manual is for all who are called to strengthen the black family.

How to Use the Black Family Ministry Manual

This manual is designed for use by pastors, staff members, a family ministry committee, and other interested laypersons.

Chapter 1 is consciousness raising. It asks "What is the Black Family?" This chapter explores the question biblically and theologically in light of past, present, and future realities. Chapter 1 will be most helpful to pastors and other leaders as they raise the congregation's awareness of the importance of ministry with families and the congregation's responsibility [call] to this ministry. This chapter is the basis for creating the climate for family ministry.

Chapters 2 and 3 give a step-by-step approach to family ministry, which includes creating the climate, organizing and building a team, diagnosing needs and interests, securing resources, program planning, implementation, evaluation, and re-diagnosis.

Chapter 4 challenges the congregation to become more effective advocates for families and identifies a gamut of advocacy techniques.

Chapter 5 offers suggestions for rituals, traditions, and celebrations that strengthen black family life.

The appendices include a compilation of replicable models of family ministry, data gathering instruments, resources for duplication, and bibliographies, as well as a list of black family ministry consultants and the denominational staff involved in the Project.

Note: Various terms are used to refer to persons of African descent. In this manual such terminology will include black and African American.

Contents

Preface

In April 1991, the National Council of Churches of Christ (NCCC) convened "Families 2000 — A Visioning Event." The event was an opportunity for professionals and nonprofessionals to project the church's mission in the twenty-first century. Resource persons and participants included sociologists, educators, economists, social service providers, Bible scholars, theologians, clergy, and laypersons. Together they explored the question, "What is the challenge to the church as it approaches the year 2000, given the present trends in family life?"

During the planning of this pivotal event, the idea emerged for a leadership training project for family ministry in black congregations. Consultants would be trained and deployed to work with congregations, and a manual or handbook would be produced.

Subsequently, over a two-year period, 1991–1993, consultants (clergy and laypersons) were trained and commissioned as black family ministry consultants to assist congregations in planning, initiating, implementing, and/or strengthening ministry with families in their congregations and communities. Although one hundred consultants were deployed to more than two hundred congregations, it was realized that this effort was but a ripple in meeting the needs of thousands of black congregations. An evaluation of the Project indicated that congregations needed ongoing assistance. This manual, which completes the Project, is designed to provide that assistance.

Louise Bates Evans
Project Director

Acknowledgments

Tremendous and grateful appreciation goes to the Lilly Endowment, Inc., without whose grant award the Leadership Training Project for Family Ministry in Black Congregations would not have been possible; to the AFL-CIO for a grant award toward the Project; to the Lutheran Brotherhood for a grant to train ECLA Consultants; to the Children's Defense Fund for technical assistance; and to Dorothy Savage of the National Council of the Churches of Christ in the U.S.A., for without her vision the Project would not have been born.

Additional appreciation goes to the participating denominations who provided staff and funding.

A special note of thanks to Candace Battle Rhodman of Business Services Etcetera for her technical support of this manual.

And many thanks to the consultants for their enthusiasm and commitment to the Project, which made this Black Family Ministry Manual possible.

CHAPTER 1

Introduction

Black Families Approaching the Twenty-first Century

The primacy of family, the importance of education, the necessity of individual enterprise and hard work, and a strong religious/spiritual foundation have been fundamental to black people's survival in America. Commitment to the family, however, has been one of the most powerful forces in black life. Because blacks have embraced a strong family ethic as central to their lives and a great majority have managed to maintain strong families, often in the face of enormous adversity, it has been documented that "Black family life has probably been the most intensely studied area of the Black experience."[1]

To be sure, sociologists and historians have offered challenging analyses of the state of black family life. Much of their commentary has been directed toward the "fragility" of the black family in America.

Writing in 1939 in *The Negro Family in the United States,* E. Franklin Frazier argued that the disorganization of the African American family was caused by slavery. Jessie Bernard, disagreeing with Frazier, ar-

gued that the conditions of black families should not be viewed merely as deviance from the white norm. The best mirror of African American life, she continued, is the African American. Andrew Billingsly viewed the goal of African American family life as the ability to produce competent individuals who can overcome some of the major aspects of their internal and external environments in order to survive, to perpetuate the race, and to make some contributions to the larger society. Robert B. Hill contended that strength and stability, not weakness and instability, are the model patterns for both low-income and middle-income African American families.[2]

In the last quarter of the twentieth century, urban living and totally urban-oriented society, with its myriad social problems, has caused fragmentation within the black family. Even the present decade is witnessing devastation and desperation among many black families. There is profound poverty among blacks, particularly in urban areas. Increasing economic pressure on the family causes all working-age family members to maintain gainful employment—a serious requirement for family survival in a time of high unemployment among black males. While twenty years ago 75 percent of black men were employed, today an astounding 45 percent of all black men do not have jobs.[3] Research suggests that black women are unable to find employed black males to marry. Thus, for many men of color, the military, the streets, or prison have become the only remaining "career" options open. Those who do not find work are generally at the lower end of the wage scale in the service and agricultural sectors of the economy.

Additional challenges to African American family life are the high rates of out-of-wedlock births and young female-headed households. Such households may contribute to a kind of "feminization of poverty." This economic perspective points to certain realities affecting many women in the United States; it addresses several distortions that directly impact black family life. First, there is the assumption that all women are equally in danger of becoming poor. The truth is that some women are poor and getting poorer, while many others are rich and getting richer. Second, this economic perspective excludes men of color, particularly African American men, from the analysis of poverty. The profile of the poor is incomplete as long as black men are excluded from the picture.[4]

Furthermore, young black males are not eligible for public welfare. Thus, the absence of any income from "legitimate" sources leaves only a limited number of options available to them. Selling drugs can become an alternative economy, providing high wages and self-esteem to young black males who are denied both in mainstream America.

Other challenges accompanying the new generation of blacks, such as the high level of welfare dependency, poor education performance, delinquency, unemployment, overwhelming crime rates, and escalating incarceration, directly affect the well-being of black family life.

Moreover, these economic, political, and social pressures, ironically, have created a family environment in which individual family members attempt to "go it alone" without regard for family solidarity. This breakdown in black family solidarity is indicative of the breakdown of community and community values. The alarming statistics provoke questions about the character and significance of family values in the black community as a whole.

This breakdown in community is no less underscored by the fact that the percentage of households where both parents are present continues to decline.

While the black family structure has historically depended upon the extended family system to provide a means for coping with special pressures and hardships, it too is currently faced with great obstacles. One indicator of this is that more and more black children are entering the foster care system.

According to K. Sue Jewell, author of *Survival of the Black Family: The Institutional Impact of U.S. Social Policy*, there is little doubt that the disintegration of black nuclear and extended families is related to liberal social policy (a government approach to poverty in the 1960s and 1970s which assumed that temporary federal intervention would effect permanent changes in the circumstances of disadvantaged Americans). Attendant problems facing black families, such as poverty, low civilian workforce participation rates for black males, and the like, are also indicators that becoming a viable member of our society is far from a reality for many black men, women, and children. The ultimate goal of liberal social policy was the transformation of black families into self-sufficient economic units akin to an "ideal" nuclear family model, which lifted up traditional male and female role expectations. These role expectations defined men as the sole breadwinners and assigned women to an affective role in which their primary responsibilites were domestic.[5]

Another factor in addition to the results of this social policy is the negative effect of a deeply held racism. Although there have been some gains for black people in the areas of education, employment, home ownership, and entrepreneurship as a result of affirmative action, these have not been significant enough to erase the overwhelming challenges that black families still face.

Consistently faced with great challenges, black families have been severely tested. One may ask: How have black families survived? What has given black families the kind of hope and fortitude to persevere? The reply most often given points to the fact that black people's strength, courage, and means of coping have come out of their religion and a spirituality nurtured through the organized church.

A More Relevant Approach to Ministry with Families

One of the most powerful truths about families is that they cannot be strong unless they are surrounded by a strong community.[6]

Black families in America have historically sought deep strength in a spiritual base through participating in the American religious enterprise, specifically the black church. To be sure, blacks have always embraced the central values of the society, augmented those values in response to the unique pressures of racism, and incorporated them into a strong religious tradition. The black church has consistently served as a stabilizing force for the black family, particularly as the family found itself in the midst of a hostile, oppressive, and racist environment.

Because of the overt segregation that existed in most of the South and the covert discrimination in the North, and because it became the sole institution owned and operated by blacks, the black church was a central force in the lives of many black people. Black churches necessarily became multifunctional community institutions. They often established their own schools and Bible societies, while serving the varied and widespread needs of a disenfranchised population. They were, and still are, one of the few places where black men and women could feel they were respected for their own talents and abilities. The community church also became one of the most important sources of leadership experience and development in the black community. The church's strength has been its prevalence, independence, and extensive outreach. Even over the past forty years, as masses of black families moved from the rural south to the urban north and west, the black church remains a strong spiritual and communications base in the community.[7]

The black church remains challenged to be at the cutting edge of the African American community's effort to shape the future of its families.

The words of W.E.B. Dubois still receive great attention today. In *The Philadelphia Negro,* published in 1899, Dubois argued that the masses of "colored people must be taught to guard the home (and family), to make it the center of social life and moral guardianship." Therefore, the church's role is of utmost importance, since "religious orientation is one of the greatest historic strengths of black families."[8]

For the past several decades, the church has focused its ministry on providing care for the family in distinctive categories—children's ministry, youth ministry, young adult and adult ministries. This approach to ministry has sought to address the changing trends in family life, as well as the specific stages of the life cycle. However, there seems to be a gap between where the church's ministry to families is today and where the church needs to be. As new challenges threaten the cohesiveness of the family as a unit, a more relevant approach to family ministry is needed. Of prime importance to a relevant approach to family ministry is intentionality. The church must be intentional in its approach, in addressing specific needs, and in its motivation for family ministry.

In order to support family life now and into the twenty-first century, the work of the church is to plan more comprehensively and holistically. Some examples of relevant approaches to family ministry include:

• the church continuing as a strong "extended" family for black families, in such ways as providing a practical "family" function for individual family members, both young and old alike;

• the church providing a practical "family" function of positive role models for young people, both male and female;

• the church actively being "family" for the growing number of elderly;

• the church strengthening its ability to mobilize quickly and offer assistance to families in crisis without overwhelming bureaucracy;

• the church actively involving itself in every area of black family life: economic, political, social, medical, educational, psychological, cultural, and so forth;

• the church becoming an active participant in national and state policy debates on the black family;

• the church engaging in aggressive and concrete ways to disciple black males, youth, and young adults;

• the church actively participating in broad-based community support networks;

• the church forming ecumenical partnerships to enhance black family life.

Ultimately, the responsibility of black churches is to facilitate ongoing rejuvenation and liberation for a people who are yet recovering from the aftereffects of slavery and segregation in America.

A Definition of Family

Family is defined as persons related by blood, marriage, adoption, or a binding relationship. This workable definition covers:

(a) the nuclear family—parents and children living together;

(b) the extended family—multigenerational kin or non-kin; usually three generations living together or in close proximity or close communication;

(c) step/blended families;

(d) couples without children;

(e) persons living alone who are a part of a family or a family unto themselves;

(f) single persons living together; and

(g) persons informally adopted.

The Function of the Family

An African proverb states, "It takes a whole village to raise a child." Although the importance of family historically has been promoted for the birth, nurture, and development of children, the family's functions are many: to nurture and care for all its members; to educate its members to be responsible critical thinkers; to transmit the values of their faith; and to provide a sound environment for health and wholeness. Ultimately, the family functions as one of many entities in the lives of its members.

The Definition Expanded

Several other categories of families exist for black people:

1. Persons are often informally adopted to become family: the "play mothers," the surrogate aunts, uncles, grandparents, and "kissing cousins." These relationships may or may not be intimate, but all are still considered family.

2. Family for black people also involves racial connectedness. There is a sense of kinship with other blacks because they realize they are not immune to what happens to their racial brother or sister; what happens to one black person can happen to another. Family in its broadest sense is the black community.

3. The black church is considered a family. Members of the church are children of God and brothers and sisters in Christ. Historically and theoretically, the church has been the family to embrace persons when any of the other family configurations were absent or lacking. It is the church family that gives unconditional love to hurting individuals and families when the socioeconomic and political systems impinge upon them.

Biblical and Theological Foundations

The theology or basis for *doing* family ministry is found in what one believes about God. The fact that the Bible has much to say about God's purpose for humanity suggests that God is interested in the human family.

The *need* for doing family ministry arises out of the context of the human situation. Situations of chaos, brokenness, and pain provide for the intentional and relevant application of the gospel to family needs.

The *call* to the church for being and making family is rooted in the biblical witness, particularly the New Testament description of the "household of faith."

Family Demands Relationship

The formation of family demands relationship. This formation explains why family is so closely linked with what we believe about God. Our teaching of the trinitarian nature of God: God as Father (Mother), Son, and Holy Spirit consists of a human, limited expression of God who exists in relationship.

With this belief about a relational God, we are assured that family is a part of what God intends for humanity created in the image of God. The creation stories in Genesis affirm humanity as family and as a part of God's original creation.

Diversity among Families

Despite such popular terms as "the biblical family" and "the traditional family," many family configurations are found in both the Old and New Testaments. When looking at contemporary family situations, consider some of the characteristics and the diversity of family life in the Bible:

• Hagar was the surrogate mother for Sarah (Genesis 16:2-4);

• Rebekah favored Jacob over his brother Esau (Genesis 25:28);

• Jacob's family included two wives, two maidservants, and their children; (Genesis 31);

• Joseph's estranged brothers went to him for food (Genesis 47);

• Orpah, an adult child, returned home to her parents (Ruth 1:1-14);

• Queen Esther was married to a divorced man (Esther 1–2:17);

• Abigail was a wife wiser than her husband (1 Samuel 25);

• Martha was a female head of household (John 11–12);

• Priscilla and Aquila had a dual-career marriage (Acts 18:1-4).

Love Determines the Household of Faith

The Bible insists on love rather than limiting the boundaries of family. Love for God caused some New Testament believers to place more emphasis on family relationships created by faith ties than on family kinship created by bloodline.

The followers of Jesus learned to understand what Jesus meant when he defined his principles for family relationship: "Here are my mother and my brothers! Whoever does the will of God is my brother and sister and mother" (Mark 3:34-35). Jesus wanted persons to become family based upon their love for God.

While he was on the cross, Jesus solidified the family relationship between his mother and his friend John. Even today, it is still at the foot of the cross that all who love God are made into family.

The Church Called to Be Family

Jesus' life, death, and resurrection call the church to be family. Another way of considering the faith-made family is found in Ephesians (see Ephesians 2:12-19; 5:1-2). The New Testament concept of family—household of faith—was relatively inclusive. Slaves as well as heads of households were included in this concept of family.

The Need for Family Ministry

With an informed reading of the Bible, we realize that our modern family relationships and their difficulties are not new. The contributing stressors on contemporary family life not only result from personal and family weaknesses and failures, but also from community and national injustices. Therefore, family ministry is concerned with both internal and external factors that prevent the health and welfare of families. Family ministry arises out of a need to enable all families to live, grow, and function at their greatest God-given potential.

What Is Black Family Ministry?

1. Black family ministry is ministry that *equips* black people to survive and flourish in a racist society; it is ministry that strives to empower families to claim their strengths, acknowledge their weaknesses, and actively create a healthy future for all families.

2. Black family ministry is *preventive education* that prepares family members for such tasks as responsible adult living, employment, career/vocations, marriage, parenting, and caring for the elderly and the young.

3. Black family ministry is *outreach and support* to families who hurt as a result of physical, psycho-social, economic, or political deprivation, and oppression. Family ministry helps families become interdependent as they serve one another and bear one another's burdens.

4. Black family ministry is *counseling and intervention* that can reconcile self-destructive attitudes and behaviors that threaten and destroy families, communities, and black people as a whole.

5. Black family ministry is *advocacy* on behalf of families. It requires the church and

families to become vigilant against the forces that threaten the affirming and life-giving energies of family life. Advocacy for families is grounded in the words of the prophet Micah, "And what does the Lord require of you but to do justice, and to love kindness, and to walk humbly with your God?" (Micah 6:8); in addition to the teaching of Jesus, "Truly I tell you, just as you did it to one of the least of these who are members of my family, you did it to me" (Matthew 25:40).

6. Black family ministry is *ritual and celebration*:

—Rituals and celebrations affirm God's creation of families and individuals.

—Rituals and celebrations allow time to recall and affirm the journey of the past.

—Rituals and celebrations signify time for families to recognize their strengths and grow closer together.

—Rituals and celebrations provide hope as families point toward the future.

The Goal of Family Ministry

The primary focus of family ministry is establishing and maintaining healthy families. A measure of health in black families can be ascertained by how well they contend with racism and the ambiguity of life present within their homes and in the larger community. Family wellness for black people is the ability to survive and flourish in a racist, multicultural society. Throughout history healthy black families survived and made a contribution to their race and to the country, building on their strengths rather than succumbing to adversity.

A ministry that promotes healthy families tends to be comprehensive in its function. By contrast, social service agencies tend to use the crisis-oriented model, generally treating the family after it has become dysfunctional. Comprehensive family ministry addresses the entire family life cycle and its specific challenges; there is concern for each age and stage of family life. The various stages of the life cycle present predictable challenges that can be anticipated and, in some cases, prevented.

Although family ministry seeks to help families stay well, families and individual members will probably not beat down the church door to seek help. Black families often avoid family counseling and other family services because they believe participation is an admission that their family is in trouble. Patience and perseverance have proven to be necessary virtues in providing preventive measures, support mechanisms, enrichment strategies, and avenues of celebration with a view toward family wellness.

Characteristics of a Healthy Family

From a black family perspective, the two most important characteristics of a healthy family are respect and commitment.

Respect

a. In healthy families there is respect for all family members. The family is marriage centered or, in the case of single parents, parent centered. The parents' relationship, the marriage, or the secure autonomy of the single parent should provide members with a sense of security, nurture their development, and provide the family with a stable foundation.

b. In healthy families there is respect for parental authority. Although children may share in the decision making, the final decision should come from the parent(s). Healthy parental authority promotes boundaries and limitations, prepares children for other positive authority figures in their lives, and enables the nurturing of positive self-esteem.

c. In healthy families conflict is resolved with respectful confrontation. Family members learn that conflict is inevitable and is an inherent, potentially positive aspect of any intimate relationship.

Commitment

a. In healthy families commitment is essential in nurturing the relationship. Parents are committed to each other and to the children, if any. Parents take responsibility for their children's upbringing, assuming the primary role in the children's spiritual and moral development, and even committing to some form of spiritual instruction in the home.

b. In healthy families every member is committed to making a contribution. Even children have chores for which they are not paid; for chores strengthen a child's sense of competence, responsibility, and motivation to achieve.

c. In healthy families all members (including children) commit to being accountable for their own behavior, thereby developing a clear sense of identity and autonomy.

d. In healthy families there is a commitment to the health and wellness of the family and its individual members.

A Summary of Family Ministry

Family ministry takes a comprehensive approach to supporting and strengthening families, while providing resources that undergird the family and its members through all stages of the life cycle. Family ministry is multifaceted. It includes:

a. enrichment to improve family self-image/functioning;

b. education/prevention during all phases of the life cycle;

c. intervention and support to hurting families;

d. advocacy for changes that improve the quality of life for families;

e. rituals and celebrations to strengthen the intergenerational family;

f. a systems approach in empowering families to interact with other systems. For example, a comprehensive systems approach to family ministry would not only seek to prevent family discord, school dropouts, violence, teen parenthood, unemployment, and underemployment but would also provide intervention and supportive services/programs to persons who are experiencing these challenges/crises.

Family ministry is grounded in the Christian faith, expressing hope, solid values, and service to all families.

Family Ministry Is Proclaiming God's Love for Families through:

Enrichment

Marriage Enrichment
Family Clusters
Parent to Parent
Mentoring
Respite caregivers
Employment counseling
Recreational activities

Education

Parenting skills
Stages of development
Preparation for marriage
Communication skills
Interpersonal relationship
Conflict resolution
Loss and letting go
Care for young and elderly
History and heritage
Ending family violence

Intervention/Counseling

Pastoral counseling/referral
Peer counseling
AA/NA groups
Counseling in legal confrontations
Support groups for divorced, victims, bereaved, new parents, children, youth

Advocacy

Promoting a family friendly congregation and schedule
Advocating for social change that elevates the quality of life
Advocating for a drug-free and violence-free community

Rituals and Celebrations

Worship service/family worship in the home
Reunions/homecomings/anniversaries
Birthdays/recognitions
Weddings/funerals
Parent-child dedications
History and heritage
Rites of passage
Juneteenth/Kwanza
Family trips/tours
Storytelling

1. Wade W. Nobles and Goddard L. Lawford, *Understanding the Black Family: A Guide for Scholarship and Research* (San Francisco: The Institute for the Advanced Study of Black Family Life and Culture, Inc., 1984), 2.

2. Robert Staples, *The Black Family: Essays and Studies* (California: Wadsworth Publishing Company, 1994), 6.

3. Ibid., 248.

4. Ibid., 245.

5. K. Sue Jewell, *Survival of the Black Family: The Institutional Impact of U.S. Social Policy* (New York: Praeger Publishers, 1988), 90.

6. Andrew Billingsley, *Climbing Jacob's Ladder* (New York: Simon and Schuster, 1992), 70.

7. Nancy Boyd-Franklin, *Black Families in Therapy: A Multisystems Approach* (New York: The Guilford Press, 1989), 81.

8. Billingsley, *Climbing Jacob's Ladder*, 349.

CHAPTER 2

Creating the Climate for Family Ministry

The church that recognizes its responsibility to support and strengthen families may not know how to get started. The process begins with creating the climate in the congregation. This involves raising the congregation's awareness of family ministry (see Activities to Raise Awareness, page 12), gaining an understanding of ministry with families, and organizing the team to coordinate family ministry.

To begin the process, consider the following questions:

•How do individuals in the congregation relate with one another?

•Who are the present leaders in the church, formal and informal?

•Is there conflict within the congregation at the present time?

•How is conflict handled in the congregation so that work gets done?

•What are the value systems that exist within the congregation?

Consideration of these kinds of questions assists in evaluating the current realities in the congregation.

Evaluating Current Realities

There are three phases in creating the climate and setting the stage for family ministry in the congregation:

PHASE 1:
Assessing the Vision of the Pastor/Minister

This phase of creating the climate provides guidance in observing the position of the pastor/minister concerning family ministry.

When "family ministry" is mentioned to pastors, one of two responses is generally offered: "Of course we have family ministry," and he or she names the family-night programs and the potluck dinners; or the pastor will throw up his or her hands in despair and ask, "How can I do any more? I am on call now to families twenty-four hours a day!"

A comprehensive approach to ministry with families goes beyond the family-night programs and the potluck dinners. It is an effort that spreads the task of supporting and strengthening families throughout the congregation rather than placing the total responsibility on the pastor/minister. The congregation becomes the family of God ministering with and to families.

The Role of the Pastor/Minister

(The title pastor/minister is used here to include lay leaders and other persons who may be responsible for the task of family ministry.)

1. The pastor/minister is the spiritual leader of the congregation, who reminds the congregation of God's call to be in relationship with one another.

2. The pastor/minister raises the consciousness of the congregation by relating the current realities of family life and proclaiming the possibilities for healing the family.

3. The pastor/minister becomes an enabler—one who finds alternative ways to minister with families using a one-to-one approach, support groups, and/or an education/enrichment model.

4. The pastor/minister is a change agent, a catalyst who empowers the congregation to minister to one another. The pastor/minister sets the tone, enabling the congregation to become the caring family of God.

5. The pastor/minister identifies the person(s) who will assist in coordinating the ministry, delegates responsibilities, and supports the person's work.

6. The pastor/minister is open to new ways of ministry, especially through networking with other pastors, congregations, and community agencies.

PHASE 2:
Evaluating the Existing Climate

This phase of creating the climate provides an opportunity to evaluate where the congregation is and where it wants to be. As a group exercise, answer the following questions:

1. How does your church currently support family ministry?

2. In worship services where family themes are presented and preached, how does your church emphasize those themes? Negatively or positively?

3. In what ways does your church schedule/calendar consider family needs?

4. How well does your church's Christian education program enhance family life as well as personal spiritual growth?

5. What kind of resources are provided for doing family ministry?

6. Is there an evaluation mechanism in place to assess family ministry?

PHASE 3:
Determining the Congregation's Potential

This phase of creating the climate facilitates the process of determining what the church wants to accomplish. Is the congregation ready and willing to:

•Make strengthening and supporting families and family life a priority?

•Take available resources seriously?

•Select one or more persons to assume leadership in developing a Family Enrichment Ministry?

•Become sensitized to family needs?

•Reevaluate the demands of church life and family life?

Activities to Raise Awareness

Congregational awareness is key in creating a climate for family ministry. Since churches do not start from point zero, engaging in certain activities will help to raise the congregation's awareness. The following are some suggested activities.

1. The month of May has been designated as "Family Month" in many denominations. Plan special activities during that time. The pastor can also emphasize family-life issues sermonically (for sermon ideas, see Appendix A).

2. Ask all persons in the congregation to share family snapshots. Create a montage in an area that gets a lot of traffic, perhaps the fellowship hall or the area near the sanctuary.

3. Add to the montage snapshots from intergenerational church gatherings and from neighborhood walks.

4. Collect and display pictures from *Ebony, American Visions*, and other magazines and posters from the Children's Defense Fund.

5. Start a reading room, offering poetry, prose, fiction, and nonfiction by and about African Americans. Include artwork by black artists and musicians.

6. Look at the church calendar of scheduled activities. Avoid overscheduling that fractures the family unit. Plan more intergenerational activities—become a "family friendly" church.

7. Help children to grow in the faith by regularly including them as leaders and helpers in the worship service.

8. Celebrate families by recognizing one family each month during the year. Continue this recognition until all persons in the church have been recognized. Create extended families as desired to include single persons.

9. Launch new projects in family ministry and celebrate accomplishments with potluck dinners.

10. Post news articles about family life on two bulletin boards: on one post articles that are uplifting; on the other post articles that present challenges in family life. Display local and national examples.

Organizing for Family Ministry

At this point, the focus turns to organizing personnel to coordinate family ministry. Knowledge of team building and group dynamics is essential in creating the right climate. The success of a ministry with families depends upon the senior pastor's commitment to the ministry and the leadership of the designated director/coordinator of the ministry. The congregation perceives the pastor's commitment through the sermons preached, but mostly through his/her encouragement to the director/coordinator and the family ministry team. (See Appendix B for an example of an organizational chart for family ministry.)

The Role of the Director / Coordinator

The director/coordinator leads the family ministry team that assists the congregation in planning and shaping its ministry. The director/coordinator, who is usually selected by the pastor, may be a professional or a layperson with a devotion to serving others. Whatever method is used in selecting a person or persons to lead the team, commitment to family ministry is essential. A Leadership Covenant, such as the one provided in this chapter (which may be adapted to your specific situation), can be used to demonstrate the importance of such a commitment.

Finally, family ministry must be included in the congregation's budget. A congregation will support what it values. The director/coordinator's position, which often begins as a volunteer position, should become a compensated responsibility similar to that of the organist/musician. Even minimal compensation makes the statement that "your contribution is valuable to us."

Desirable Characteristics of the Director/Coordinator

- strong supporter of families
- affirms diversity/nonjudgmental
- dreamer/goalsetter/visionary
- informed/willing to learn/open-minded
- committed to follow through
- assertive/will take a stand
- not easily discouraged/not afraid to start again
- inspirational/inspires others
- good leader/good communicator/develops leadership in others
- believes that through God all things are possible
- above all, is very patient.

Leadership Covenant

As a leader of the church striving to set a spiritual example for others, I will to the best of my ability commit myself to:

—be an active leader of family ministries.

—participate actively in the duties of my board and committees and attend the necessary meetings. If I am unable to fulfill an obligation, I further commit myself to make proper notification to the pastor (or other designated person).

—attend regularly all worship services, including morning and evening services each Sunday, and put a high priority on attending Sunday church school, Bible study, and/or prayer meeting.

—give sacrificially of my treasure to the work of the Lord in this church through the tithing system.

—be confidential in matters pertaining to my board and committee.

If at any time I can no longer uphold this covenant of Christian leadership, I will cheerfully relinquish my position.

Signature

Building the Team

The family ministry team is made up of representatives from standing congregational groups: the women's missionary group, the church school, youth fellowship, the men's group, the senior citizens' group, the deacons, and the church board. Also add to the team at-large members and persons from the congregation who do not represent an organized group but have an interest in serving in this ministry.

Choosing Team Members

Team members need specific talents:

a. They must be able to articulate the needs and concerns of the constituency they represent, while working with other team members to implement a comprehensive family ministry program. They need to be visionaries with a multifocused rather than a single-focused vision.

b. They must be enthusiastic communicators, able to convey ideas to the congregation as a whole. Their enthusiasm for family ministry should be sincere, caring, and contagious to the extent that others catch the spirit and are motivated and mobilized.

c. They must have knowledge and proven expertise or practical life skills in certain needed areas such as parenting, marriage, friendship, community service, and so on. Other needed expertise includes teaching, health and human services, policy making, law enforcement, business, and fundraising. Every congregation has persons who either fall into these categories or have contact with people who do.

Be creative when forming the family-ministry team. Successful family-ministry programs utilize resources within the congregation. The more the congregation is involved, the greater their ownership and investment and the stronger the ministry.

Team/Group Dynamics

Whenever individuals work together in a group, differences will arise. Sometimes the result is serious conflict. Some of the contributing factors to conflict are personality clashes, power struggles, a stressful environment, unreasonable expectations, and unclear goals. However, there are healthy and helpful methods of conflict resolution. The following are suggestions for preventing unnecessary conflict:

1. Start every meeting with prayer and meditation on a passage of Scripture.
2. Develop a good working theology of conflict (refer to Acts 15).
3. Become aware of one's own preferred and alternate methods of handling conflict.
4. Learn ways of developing and implementing conflict intervention techniques.
5. Utilize the resources of one's church tradition and the Christian faith in conflict intervention/resolution.

Six Steps to Conflict Management

1. Identify and define the conflict.
2. Brainstorm solutions to the conflict.
3. Evaluate the solutions.
4. Choose a solution.
5. Implement the solution.
6. Do a follow-up evaluation.

Guidelines for Responding to Conflict

1. Accept conflicts as natural.
2. Disagree with ideas, not with people.
3. When defining an issue or problem, always define it as shared.
4. Identify and focus on the most important central issues to the conflict.
5. Don't polarize the conflicting positions.
6. Don't compromise too quickly.
7. If you are not centrally involved in a conflict, be cautious when supporting one view over another.

Overcoming Resistance

A new ministry often encounters great resistance, especially when there are misconceptions. Below are several excuses often given in relation to family ministry, followed by appropriate responses that may prove helpful.

Excuse: This is not ministry, and it does not belong in the church.

Response: The church is the place where one becomes who he/she is in relation to God and others. Family ministry is a ministry of hope.

Excuse: We pay the pastor to do family ministry; it is his/her responsibility. The pastor says, "I am overworked; I cannot see all the families who need help."

Response: This is a ministry that empowers members of the congregation to share in ministry with the pastor. Families are empowered to love and support one another in new ways.

Excuse: Our families are not dysfunctional; why do we need family ministry?

Response: Your church will benefit from family enrichment programs because all families want to be strengthened and enriched.

Excuse: If you are a Christian, you won't have family problems.

Response: You are right to think that the church helps families to address their problems, but families also experience difficulties that are the result of external forces and not a result of a lack of faith.

Excuse: What will this new ministry cost? We don't have any money.

Response: The commitment to family ministry is more important than money. Since we value what we pay for, a church that values families will move toward including family ministry in the budget. Many programs can begin without money, for example: *support groups* for parents, for divorced persons and their children, and for other grieving persons; *mentoring groups*, providing "big sisters/brothers," foster grandparents, and faith partners; *celebrations*, such as family nights, potluck dinners, reunions, and trips; *service projects*, intergenerational volunteering, and work projects.

CHAPTER 3

Steps toward a Comprehensive Family Ministry

A Call to Ministry

Historically, the church has been the place where black people have experienced unconditional, positive regard. As the church is called to be that place for families, the basic concerns of the church's ministry are the maintenance of intrinsic moral, ethical, and spiritual values and the sanctity of the family bond.

In his book *Roots of a Black Future*, Dr. J. Deotis Roberts states, "Since Black families are the source of the Black church's life and growth, the measure of its ministry to Black families will determine the quality of its mission."[1]

Survival of black families and the black church requires cooperative efforts and vision. If the awesome problems facing black families will ever be remedied, families and the church must redefine and reexamine their gifts and strengths in order to retool for an enhanced family ministry.

Program Planning

The ability to make a real difference in the lives of families is the result of intentional planning and hard work. A real difference is visible change in opportunity, care, relationships, and the overall quality of life. A real difference brings results for particular people in particular places. Throughout biblical, cultural, and social histories, lives have been transformed, relationships set right, and new structures created because persons have been called and empowered to effect change.

Program planning is one of the intentional ways of effecting change. It has often been said that "to fail to plan is to plan to fail." Planning for family ministry requires an assessment of the needs and interests within the congregation and the community. Assessing is taking stock of who you are, where you are, and what you have going for yourself. Consider the following questions in planning a program for family ministry:

- Who are we?
- Where are we?
- Where are the hurts?
- Where are the hopes?
- Where are the opportunities?

•Where are the challenges?

•What are the problems/issues?

Before we get from here to there, we must know who we are and where we are. Assess your church's ministry to and with families by engaging in the following exercises. (For the best results, all exercises in this chapter should be done in a group setting with the responses being recorded on newsprint. If possible, display all newsprint sheets so the respondents can view them clearly.)

Exercise #1:
Family-Related Ministries Already in Place

Make a list of the activities/ministries that your church is currently involved in that enrich, strengthen, and meet specific needs of families or individual family members. This list should include any and all events, activities, and programs that participants believe meet the needs of families or individual family members. For example: premarital counseling, midweek prayer meeting, family-night worship, after-school tutorials, weekend retreats, church anniversary celebrations, Boy Scouts and Girls Scouts, Sunday church school, Men's League, and so forth. The list can be as long as is needed.

Needs-Oriented Planning

All program development begins with some kind of need. The need can be stated or not stated. A "felt" need is what we think, believe, feel, or understand about ourselves and others (for example, my family). An "ascribed" need is what an observer believes is needed. Planning ministry around ascribed needs can be risky because observations may only be superficial.

Assess the needs of the congregation as well as the needs of the community in which the congregation is located. Be sure to ask as a congregation: Whose needs are we trying to meet? Ministries are sometimes initiated without first determining the "real" needs to be met.

Exercise #2:
Responding to the Critical Question

What do you perceive to be the greatest challenge/problem confronting the black family?

Make a list of responses from the above question. Ask each and every participant to respond, reassuring them that there are no right or wrong answers. They should be urged not to judge others' responses or place any limitations on their own responses. Responses can also develop from another's responses. (Be sure to record all responses on newsprint and display the newsprint sheets.)

Please note: Some of these replies may seem humorous!

After listing all responses to the Critical Question, make a comparison between the lists recorded on newsprint from Exercise #1 and Exercise #2. As you compare the two lists, observe your congregation's current family-related ministries in relationship to the challenges/problems confronting the black family. How many of the problems listed in Exercise #2 are addressed through the ministries listed in Exercise #1?

For many congregations, there is a large gap between what the problems are and how the congregations seek to address those problems. The problems confronting black families may be considered an "itch." The family-related ministries that the congregation is already engaged in may be considered a "scratch." Is your congregation "scratching" where black families are "itching"?

Data Gathering

To assist in needs-oriented planning, data gathering is necessary. Gathering data is the process of obtaining information about the needs that will assist the congregation in planning an effective family ministry. Data gathering serves three purposes:

- It assists in establishing good goals.
- It helps in locating the most effective means for doing ministry.
- It assists in evaluating the work.

(One particular method of gathering data follows in Exercise #3; other methods, for example, congregational, opinion, and family needs and interests surveys, are included in Appendix A).

Exercise #3:
Investigative Reporting

Investigative reporting is a data gathering technique used to assess the needs in the community. It begins with a walking tour of the community and climaxes with a report of findings to the planning group. It is observing and reporting.

Begin by appointing teams consisting of three or more persons who will gather data in the specific areas of the community listed below and report back at a planning meeting. Each team can list its findings (location, conditions, what's available, how many, and so forth) on newsprint and give a five-minute report to the planning group. This information will be useful in assessing the needs in the community. Five teams are listed here; other teams may be added if needed.

Children and Schools

1. Attendance figures of neighborhood school or those who get bused out of neighborhood

2. Number of before- and after-school care programs

3. Educational enrichment/tutoring/extra-curricular opportunities

4. High school graduation/drop-out rate/suspensions.

Family and Children's Services

1. Availability of child care, health care, and social services

2. Utilization of the services—why or why not?

3. Security/police patrol/precincts.

Churches and Recreation

1. Number of churches and history of co-operation

2. Types and availability of recreational facilities

3. List existing programs/services, utilization, perceived needs.

Business and Industry

1. Types of businesses in community

2. Employment opportunities

3. Black-owned and operated businesses

4. Indicators of unemployment

5. Availability of supermarkets and shopping centers.

Undesirable Conditions

1. Evidence of drug abuse and sales

2. Loitering

3. Liquor stores (location) and "Variety Stores"

4. Abandoned and vacant housing

5. Poor conditions of environment.

Special Notes on Needs Assessments

- Surveys are generally not as good as a participatory process and personal interviews.

• Collect right information. Right information aids in making right decisions.

• Make sure the data collected is of high quality and highly reliable.

• Remember, good information is vital for good planning and is to be used wisely for good purposes.

Exercise #4:
Identifying the Real Concerns

1. Determine by consensus which are the real concerns. Do this by observing similarities between the lists made in Exercise #2 and Exercise #3. Is there an overlap of the problems confronting black families?

2. Spend adequate time in prayer and serious thought about where to make a real difference. Choose specific issues that are solvable. Don't try to cover the whole world!

3. Prioritize the concerns. Then determine which concern(s) will be addressed. The group should select one to three issues/concerns.

4. Brainstorm solutions to each of the concerns selected. (Don't place limitations on your solutions; come up with as many ideas as you can). Be sure to record the responses on newsprint.

Claiming and Clarifying a Vision

Claiming and clarifying a vision is hard work. Discerning God's will around particular kinds of circumstances or issues isn't always as clear to us as we'd like. Yet, moving from what our communities are to what God would have them be is the difference we must strive to make real.

Our visions grow and develop. God always calls us and reveals new challenges. As we share our visions and invite others to join us, our descriptions will become clearer and more complete. Our visions will change as we become more in tune with God's call and

our opportunities. We clarify visions so that we can act out God's love more completely in our communities.

— Marilyn Magee
Black Family Ministry National Staff Team

Claiming and clarifying a vision can be done in group work if you are willing to share your deepest hopes and to value the sharing of others. Remember: (1) The congregation needs to state its own vision. (2) The vision should come out of a mission statement.

Exercise #5:
Determining Goals

What Is a Goal?

A goal is a general, overall statement of a hoped-for result that will turn the vision into reality.

Goal setting is the planning process by which you move from where you are to where God has revealed to you that you ought to be. Goals should be broad aspirations that bring vision into reality. More than one clearly formulated goal statement may be necessary.

Example goal: The New St. James Church will assist and educate teens who are at high risk of drug abuse and premature parenthood and seek to reduce those incidences.

The goal in this example indicates that the New St. James Church believes assistance and education will reduce drug abuse and teen parenthood among teens who are at risk. This goal is realistic, worthwhile, and attainable.

What means of assistance and educational strategies will they use? How will they identify "teens at high risk"?

Here are two generalizations used in identifying high risk teens:

• Boys and girls who are unemployed

and/or out of school are at risk of drug abuse and premature parenthood;

• Teenagers with low self-esteem and no goals are at risk of drug abuse and premature parenthood;

Other factors that place children and teens at risk of drug abuse and premature parenthood are:

1. Inadequate supervision at home
2. Dysfunctional families with multiple problems
3. Low self-esteem and no goals/dreams
4. Out of school and unemployed
5. Decaying neighborhoods
6. Limited interaction with the community of faith (church)
7. Limited vision of alternatives and choices
8. Limited outlets for recreation
9. Lack of role models and appropriate authority figures
10. Feelings of inadequacy and hopelessness.

Since adolescence is a challenging period of development for young people seeking self-identity and self-expression, *all teens* are "at risk" and will benefit from assistance and education.

After determining your goal(s), decide the steps that are necessary for accomplishing the goal. These are the objectives.

Exercise #6:
Setting Objectives

An objective is a specific statement of intent, which when accomplished will move you closer to the goal. Objectives become "road maps" for activities and tasks that must be done. It is likely that more than one objective will be needed to accomplish the goal.

Objectives are set by filling in the following:

Who _____

Will do what _____
By when _____
Where _____
Why _____

Example objective from the previous listed goal:

The New St. James Church Family Ministry Team will identify, assist, and educate high-risk teens in the congregation and in the community, beginning August 1, in order to break the cycle of despair.

Additional Objectives

The Family Ministry Team will provide:

1. assistance to preteens and teenagers through a hotline, administered by select volunteer parents who will advise and refer to available resources.
2. educational programs and resources that enhance self-esteem and promote decision making and responsible goal setting (for example, Life Planning Series).
3. job training and placement for summer and out-of-school youth (for example, work with community agencies).
4. an advocacy plan in an effort to reclaim the neighborhood from destructive forces that create despair.

Exercise #7:
Developing a Budget:

Prepare a proposed budget. Include start-up costs, operational expenses, and costs for special events. Include publicity expenses and other expected and unexpected costs. Investigate potential sources of funding.

If the program requires staffing, equipment, and other costly items, be open to involving other agencies, programs, and organizations that can provide adequate assistance and services.

Program/Project Action Plan

An action plan provides the details for the who, what, when, where, and how much involved in your plans. Goals and objectives are good, but they will not spell out the various tasks. A "task" is a planned step necessary to accomplish the desired objective. There are always many tasks! Other parts of the action plan include various resources that are needed, timetables and schedules, and evaluation and assessment methods.

Use the three Program/Project Action Plan sheets in Appendix A to develop a concrete plan of action.

Implementing the Program

Implementing family ministry is a cooperative effort. Now that the action plans are completed, secure the commitment to act! The pastor gives support and permission to start the ministry. The director/coordinator guides the Family Ministry Team that helps the congregation shape its ministry. Ministry then becomes a congregational endeavor that strengthens and supports families in the church and in the community.

Monitoring the Program

Implementation includes having a way of monitoring the action plan. By reviewing the following questions, you can adequately monitor the action plan. Refer to the Program/Project Action Plan Timeline as you review the following questions:

- Are we faithful to the tasks? Why or why not?
- Are we on target?
- Are the timelines and schedules in place?
- Do we need to make adjustments?

Evaluating the Program

Determine how the program should be evaluated and develop an evaluation instrument during the planning process. Remember that the purpose of evaluation is to assess the accomplishments of goals, to gather data, to determine new objectives, and/or to project new goals.

Celebrations

Do not forget to celebrate! Celebrate the accomplishments that have been made, even if they seem small. Pay tribute to those who put in effort, time, and money. Don't forget the little things. People may serve because they see service as their ministry, but it helps to know that others appreciate both them as persons and the effort they put into the work.

---

1. J. Deotis Roberts, *Roots of a Black Future: Family and Church* (Philadelphia: Westminister, 1980), 132.

CHAPTER 4

Being Advocates for Families

What Is Advocacy?

Advocacy is the activity of pleading the cause or standing up for someone; it is giving active support on behalf of a person or persons. Advocacy is raising one's voice to make a difference.

Advocacy is the process that works toward *change* for the good of another:

• Advocacy is one person defending the rights of another person.

• Advocacy is a group of people recognizing the needs of one person or a group of persons and working to get those needs met.

• Advocacy is a church working to change public policies to improve the quality of life of its families and community.

As an advocate for families, your congregation can voice your concerns in the state legislature and on Capitol Hill. You can make a difference for families!

Why Advocate?

Advocates are similar to lobbyists in state legislatures or in Congress in that lobbyists work to get laws passed or a vote made in favor of their special interests. The difference between advocates and lobbyists is that advocates work (usually for no personal profit) on behalf of other people to promote positive legislation or defeat destructive legislation.

Advocates use information to educate legislators and others in order to win their support. Advocates tell legislators why they believe their solutions will work. Advocates use numbers to demonstrate that a significant portion of the population (voters, community leaders, and so on) is also interested in the issue. Success for advocates is found in two ways (sometimes three): in information and in numbers (and in an occasional threat of legal action).

Family ministry calls the church to be advocates for families. The issues that threaten the health and welfare of black families—poverty, homelessness, poor health care, unemployment, pollution, and so forth—can be changed with active church support speaking out against these issues.

As advocates for families, congregations can become a visible force to make changes. Elected officials hold their positions because the members of congregations elect them. They are the members' "employees" in the state legislatures and in Congress, and they need votes and feedback to represent the churches' best interests. In advocacy, congregations have great power waiting to be used to enhance the quality of life for black families.

The Tools of Advocacy

Sending a Letter to Congress

Many people believe that writing a letter to their legislator will not make much of a difference, but it does. Members of Congress usually receive one hundred letters or less on any one issue. One letter out of a hundred can make a difference.

Letter writing works. Letters are most effective if they are timely, sincere, and personalized. They are also helpful because they can provide legislators with useful information.

When to Write a Letter

Write anytime you are concerned about an issue. The best times to send a letter are when legislation is being written, when hearings are being held, or when a vote is about to take place.

How and What to Write

Be brief. Address only one issue. A letter need not be longer than four or five sentences.

Be specific. If you are writing about specific legislation, include its bill number in the title.

Write your own letter, adapting a sample letter as appropriate. Form letters do not receive the same attention as individually written letters.

Be positive and constructive. Try to say something complimentary in the first paragraph. It is just as important to thank your legislator for voting the right way as to criticize him or her for voting the wrong way.

Say in your own words why the legislation matters to you and to families. Clearly state your reason for supporting or opposing the bill or issue you are writing about.

If you have particular knowledge or expertise, describe it. Relating the bill to local or state conditions is especially effective.

If you wish, feel free to include a copy of a report, newsletter story, or local survey to support your arguments. Don't presume that the legislator is aware of such information, even if you think it is common knowledge.

Be sure to sign your name legibly and include your address so that your representative or senator can respond and so that there is a record of your letter on file.

Ask Others to Write Letters

Just as one letter is effective, thirty letters on the same issue are even better. Getting others to write to members of Congress or state legislators is not as hard as it seems. You can make a party out of it. Take some inexpensive writing paper and envelopes to a meeting at your church, your service organization, your office, or anywhere you gather with other people. Write the letters together. In ten to fifteen minutes you will end up with a considerable amount of mail.

Telephoning the Office of Your Senator/Representative

Telephone calls are a useful and effective means of reaching your Congress member's office in Washington, D.C., or your state legislator. Calls are useful when a vote has been scheduled at short notice and when there is not enough time to write a letter.

Where to Call

In Washington, D.C., the Capitol Hill

Switchboard number is (202) 224-3121, and the operator will connect you with the correct office. For their local offices, look up the number in your local telephone book under U.S. Government. It is better to dial the office direct if you know the number (it saves money, too).

What to Say When You Call

- Identify yourself by name and address or hometown;
- Identify the bill by name and number;
- Briefly state your position and explain what you want;
- Ask for your legislator's view on the bill; be firm but polite in obtaining a commitment to vote;
- Request that your call be referred to the legislator; point out that you are calling in reference to a vote that is about to happen.

Sending Mailgrams, Telegrams, or Public Opinion Messages

When time is critical, a telegram, mailgram, or public opinion message may be used. Wire services are simple, fast, and direct; and they have a real impact. Most groups, however, have found using wire services too complicated and hard to monitor. Your group must decide which method best meets your needs.

The advantage of using a wire service is that it can catch a legislator's attention, especially when organized in such a way that he

Sample Letter to Legislators

Date

The Honorable_____   OR   The Honorable_____
United States Senate   United States House of Representatives
Washington, DC 20510   Washington, DC 20510

Dear Senator/Representative:

I urge you to vote for (or *against*) SB (#) a bill to _____ that will be voted on (date).

I support (*or oppose*) this bill because (then write 1-3 paragraphs explaining your reason for opposing or supporting the bill).

Thank you for your support on this issue.

Sincerely,

(Your name)
(Your address)

or she receives many on the same day. The fact that you have kept track of the legislation to the point that you know when a crucial time arrives impresses the legislator. They assume, and rightly so, that most of their constituents are not interested enough in the process to watch it that closely.

When to Use the Wire Service

• Just before a vote to reinforce what you have previously said in a letter or meeting

• In concert with last-minute phone calls to a legislator who needs constituent pressure

• When a bill has been brought to the floor unexpectedly (bypassing the committee process)

• When a bill has been added onto another bill as an amendment or rider.

What Churches Can Do

The following are a few ideas that local churches can use to become advocates for families, especially for children. The ideas come from the Children's Defense Fund's publication *Welcome the Child, A Church Guide to Child Advocacy*.

1. Churches and religious institutions, given their stature in the community, are well suited to offer formalized family support programs, for example, referrals for family services via a "pastoral care center":

• Employment/job referral service/unemployment "insurance" or safety net
• Health services
• Continuing education
• Parental guidance
• Crisis intervention/family counseling
• Mentoring programs
• Sites for blood banks, bookmobiles, career fairs. . . .

2. Make children a top priority for financial and volunteer resources. Take special collections for children and families. Try a collection for health care, homelessness, or some issue not often addressed by the church. Another alternative would be to devote a specified fraction of all offerings to kids. Focus volunteer efforts on bettering conditions of local children and families.

3. Have a "Children's Day" to focus attention on the needs of children. Consider substantive issues instead of putting children on display. Other notes or prayers might be designed for celebration at critical points in children's development.

4. Encourage members to advocate for children, and keep them apprised of what they can do to help children on a local, state, and national level. A religious network might support a single national, state, and local children's policy/funding goal each year.

5. Where the church is affiliated with a school, make every effort to ensure adequate funding and fiscally prudent long-range planning. Given the state of many inner-city public schools, private religious-affiliated education is often the only opportunity for getting a quality education. Every effort must be made to make it affordable and give parents a choice.

6. Ensure that attending church is relevant to children on some level. Be sure to offer youth and family ministry.

7. Offer before/after-school programs. These should be related to education, not simply child care. Tutoring programs, adult literacy and parent education efforts, recreation, youth services, and other family and community learning and counseling center initiatives are a few suggestions.

Moments in Black America

Every 101 seconds a black infant is born into poverty.

Every 3 minutes a black infant is born to a teenage mother.

Every 12 minutes a black infant is born to a teenage mother who already had a child.

Every 6 minutes a black infant is born with a low birth weight (below 5 pounds, 8 ounces).

Every 28 minutes a black infant is born with very low birth weight (below 3 pounds, 5 ounces).

Every 74 seconds a black infant is born to an unmarried mother.

Every 3 minutes a black infant is born to a mother who is not a high school graduate.

Every 13 minutes a black infant is born to a mother who is a 4-year-college graduate.

Every 7 minutes a black infant is born to a mother who received late or no prenatal care.

Every 2 minutes a black 15-19-year-old woman becomes sexually active for the first time.

Every 2 minutes a black 15-19-year-old woman becomes pregnant.

Every 5 minutes a black 15-19-year-old woman aborts.

Every 46 minutes a black infant dies in the first year of life.

Every 37 hours a black child under 5 is murdered.

Every 9 hours a black youth 15-19 is murdered.

Every 5 hours a black young adult 20-24 is murdered.

Every 8 seconds of the school day a black public school student is suspended.

Every 13 seconds of the school day a black public school student is corporally punished.

Every 41 seconds of the school day a black student drops out of school.[1]

Advocacy Groups to Contact

BLACK CHILD DEVELOPMENT INSTITUTE
1463 Rhode Island Avenue, NW
Washington, DC 20005

BREAD FOR THE WORLD
802 Rhode Island Avenue, NE
Washington, DC 20018
(202) 269-0200

CHILDREN'S DEFENSE FUND
25 E Street, NW
Washington, DC 20001
(202) 628-8787

INTERFAITH IMPACT
100 Maryland Avenue, NE
Washington, DC 20002
(202) 544-8636

THE INSTITUTE FOR PEACE AND JUSTICE
4144 Lindell #122
St. Louis, MO 63108
(314) 533-4445

RESULTS
236 Massachusetts Avenue, NE, Suite 300
Washington, DC 20002
(202) 543-9340
(202) 546-3228

A Resource Advocacy Manual

So You Want to Make a Difference by Nancy Amidei is a policy advocacy manual. To order a copy, call (202) 234-8494.

---

1. Kathleen A. Guy, *Welcome the Child: A Child Advocacy Guide for Churches* (Washington, D.C.: Children's Defense Fund, 1990).

CHAPTER 5

Rituals and Celebrations for Family Ministry

Rituals are everyday, ordinary habits and procedures that families do together, like picking up or dropping off children at school, gathering together for mealtime, reciting grace before meals, and brushing teeth at bedtime.

- Rituals provide a rhythm that holds the family together.
- Rituals help to promote healthy cohesiveness among family members.
- Rituals facilitate the positive nurturing and development of all family members, particularly children; for example, setting aside reading time can promote the ritual of a scheduled bedtime for children.

Celebrations are special observances or traditions that honor significant happenings in family and community life: weddings, anniversaries, birthdays, graduations, and so on.

- Celebrations provide special occasions for formal or informal gatherings.
- Celebrations keep alive honored traditions in family and community life.
- Celebrations promote a balanced perspective on wholesome family life.

Described on the following pages are three selected rituals and celebrations that are significant in the lives of many black families: storytelling, the Juneteenth Celebration, and family worship in the home.

Storytelling

Storytelling is one of the oldest art forms in the world. It has been called the first conscious form of literary communication. Storytelling is the passing on of history, stories, legends, tales, and so forth, through an oral tradition.

The significance of telling stories has been crucial in the lives of black people and among other ethnic groups as well. The African American oral tradition originated with the creation of civilization in Africa.

Storytelling:
- provides dramatic joy
- fosters a sense of humor
- develops the imagination

• informs about certain tendencies in human nature

  • promotes an ideal action or behavior

  • presents a particular historical perspective.

Storytelling was brought into America by African captives and was common among the early descendants in the family and in the church. The telling of stories became imperative during slavery as a means of keeping alive African history and tradition.

Even today in the true African tradition, the mastery of the spoken word still overshadows the writing of the stories that need to be told. Many storytellers comment that speaking the stories is not more important than writing them down but is sometimes more effective.

Families that engage in storytelling value and affirm their past and present history, enrich the lives of family members, and inspire the future of their children. Described below are three exercises to enhance the telling of family stories.

Exercise #1:
Storytelling through a Family Book

Keep a scrapbook of your family activities: vacations that you take, souvenirs, pictures of children's artwork, snapshots, and brief written descriptions of some of the activities. Let the children help with the book, even if they can only scribble! You can use this book as you tell family stories.

Exercise #2:
Storytelling to Celebrate the Tradition

If your family is planning a visit with the grandparents or great-grandparents, plan some time to talk to them (in the presence of your children) about some of the traditions they remember. The traditions might be about specific holidays, special food, par-ticular people, favorite stories or lessons they learned in their childhood. Then as a family, you might want to choose one or two of the traditions that you could incorporate into your own family life.

Exercise #3:
Storytelling by Interviewing Family Members

This is a simple exercise for children. Using a tape recorder, they can interview family members on tape, asking questions about time and place of birth, family traditions, significant happenings during childhood, friends, teachers, jobs held, and so forth.

Juneteenth

On January 31, 1865, Congress passed the Thirteenth Amendment abolishing slavery throughout all of the United States and areas subject to its jurisdiction. This amendment was necessary because the Emancipation Proclamation outlawed slavery only in the eleven states that had seceded from the Union, not throughout the whole country.

The message of freedom from slavery reached different parts of America on various dates between 1863 and 1865. Texas slaves did not know about the Emancipation Proclamation that freed them in 1863 until after the Civil War ended in 1865. It was on June 19, 1865, that General Gordon Granger landed near Galveston, Texas, with the news that all slaves were free by the Thirteenth Amendment.

"Juneteenth" derived its name from that date—June 19th. The celebration is also referred to as "Emancipation Day," "Emancipation Celebration," "Freedom Day," and "Jun—Jun."

Today Juneteenth is observed all across the country from January to September. The specific date of celebration may indicate when the message of freedom reached different parts of the country, or the date when the enforcement of freedom actually reached black slaves in a particular area. Juneteenth is most popular in Texas and other parts of the deep South. Currently, Texas is the only state to make it a legal holiday.

Juneteenth serves as a reminder of the injustice of slavery, but also celebrates what black people have accomplished since the time of slavery.

How to Celebrate Juneteenth

This should be a day of fun, food, family, music, and dancing. The aim is to celebrate the day with great joy as our ancestors did when they learned of their freedom. Some celebrations have included:
- Family picnics
- Worship/thanksgiving services at church
- Block/community parties
- Sports events
- Talent contests/beauty pageants
- Breakfast meetings
- Luncheons/dinners

In many regions the celebration still includes the reading of the freedom documents, including the Emancipation Proclamation, the Thirteenth Amendment, or a local declaration honoring freedom from slavery.

Modeling Family Worship in the Home

Seven assumptions form the basis for family worship in the home:

Assumption 1: The worship of God is primary to a wholesome life.

Assumption 2: The family is the primary human institution.

Assumption 3: The family provides us with our most basic and lasting developments as persons and as people.

Assumption 4: The family models in the home what the family values as important.

Assumption 5: A worshiping family is a wholesome family.

Assumption 6: The will of God is for our families to be wholesome.

Assumption 7: All participants involved in family worship are serious about families being wholesome.

A Definition of Worship

Worship is the surrender of our mind, body, and soul to God. Worship consists of those activities that lift all of life before the One who creates life, liberates life, and affirms life (Deuteronomy 6:5).

Theological Foundations for Family Worship

A. The first day of human existence was the sabbath day (Genesis 1:26–2:4).

B. Family worship is the foundation for communal worship (for example, Joshua 24:15).

C. Jesus redefined family within the context of the will of God (Matthew 12:46-49).

D. The early church worshiped first in homes (Acts 2:2, 46; 10; 16:11-15; 25-34; 20:20; 2 Timothy 1:3-5)

The Importance of Family Worship

Family worship is important because it:
A. Brings the family closer to God
B. Teaches the family [children and

adults] the value of nurturing their faith

C. Promotes unity and honesty within the family

D. Encourages communication among family members

E. Builds self-esteem

F. Gives focus to family goals

Hindrances to Family Worship

A. Lack of priority—Matthew 6:33
B. Lack of communication—James 1:19-20; 3:5
C. Lack of spiritual personality/or responsible spiritual leadership—Luke 10:40-42
D. Pride—Psalms 10:4; Proverbs 16:18
E. Selfishness—2 Timothy 3:2-5
F. Individualism—Judges 21:25
G. Hostility— Matthew 5:22-24; Mark 3:25
H. Unconfessed sins —Psalm 32:1-5
I. Worldliness—Psalm 49:6-8; Matthew 6:31,32
J. Guilt— Psalm 51:4

A Guide to Family Worship

To begin family worship or to strengthen it, your family will want to consider the following questions:

1. Why should my family have family worship?

Besides the biblical mandate that God commands it (Deuteronomy 6:6-9), outline some goals and reasons for engaging in family worship.

2. Who should lead family worship?

Successful family worship depends on a leader or a person who recognizes the value of this practice and is committed to maintaining it faithfully in spite of obstacles.

Although almost any believing youth or adult in the family could fill this role, the head(s) of the family should accept the responsibility for this role.

It is not necessary for the same person to initiate the family worship each time. All members of the family should be encouraged to rotate in leading the worship experience.

3. When should family worship be held?

Decide among several options; you may need to try different methods to see what works best for your family. You might:

a. set aside 15 to 30 minutes at a regular time each day;

b. have a brief devotion each day (5-10 minutes) with a longer time once a week (45-60 minutes) when you can include special activities (for example, a birthday celebration, a family talk—which is especially good with teenagers—a big family dinner, or a special project or activity;

c. set aside time (15 minutes) before a meal (breakfast or dinnertime is usually best).

4. Where should family worship be held?

A family needs a specific, regular spot for family worship.

The worship place should be where the family is least likely to be interrupted by the telephone, television, or other distractions.

Resources for family worship should be placed in the selected place ready for immediate use.

5. What resources do we need for family worship?

A Bible for every member (including the children) is necessary.

A family with small children will want

to use at least part of family worship time reading a Bible story from a children's Bible.

Resources will vary with the specific needs of the family members: a devotional booklet, a book of meditations, a tape player for music, musical instruments (guitar, keyboard, and so forth), or whatever a family chooses. (Whatever resources you choose, center attention on the Bible.)

6. What should we do in family worship?

Begin with God's Word. Select a passage from the Bible or a devotional booklet. Let someone read the passage aloud.

Encourage each family member to comment on what the Bible passage means to him or her or how it helps to direct life.

Family members may learn or review a memory verse.

Family members may sing songs, play taped music, or play an instrument.

Share experiences. Help one another recognize God's activity in their lives.

Pray together. Let each person share prayer concerns, and then have everyone pray for all requests. Or, after all prayer concerns are shared, have one person pray for one concern, another pray for another concern, until all concerns have been addressed.

Remember, family worship should include *at least* three things:

• Bible reading of a verse or passage, or a specific Bible story;

• discussion or activity related to the Scripture passage or story;

• prayer, either an opening prayer or closing prayer.

7. What can I expect as a result of family worship?

• God's reward for those families who honor God in worship;

• God's presence when families are serious about worshiping God;

• Interruptions, distractions, and discouragements in the beginning stages (but be persistent);

• Changes (be sure to evaluate and reflect on your time spent together and make needed improvements).

---

1. "Modeling Family Worship in the Home" is a workshop developed and presented by Karen J. and Alvin C. Bernstine.

Resources

Sermon Ideas

Outline #1

Titles:
1. A Message from God: "You Can't Do It All"
2. Family Ministry: God's Solution

Scripture: Exodus 18:13-25

Background: Jethro, Moses' father-in-law, brings Moses' wife and sons to the Israelite camp. Jethro stays and observes Moses at work.

Verse 14: Jethro asks, "What is this that you are doing for the people?"

Verses 15-16: Moses outlines his job description (the pastor who tries to do it all).

Verses 17-18: Jethro replies, "What you are doing is not good" (the work is too heavy for one person).

Verses 19-23: Jethro, the priest, advises Moses to establish a family ministry, delegating responsibility and training capable, honest, God-fearing people to share the load.

Verses 24-26: Moses does as Jethro advised, sharing his ministry with the chosen leaders.

Questions for consideration:
1. How does delegating responsibility, sharing in ministry, benefit both the pastor and congregation?

2. According to Jethro, what were the qualifications laypersons needed to minister to families?

3. How has God called each of us to be in ministry with one another? Where and how do we start?

Outline #2

Titles:
1. "Same O—Same O"
2. "You Are What You Teach"

Scripture: Deuteronomy 5:6-21; Deuteronomy 11:18-21

Background: Moses calls all Israel together and gives them the Ten Commandments and admonishes the Israelites to follow the commandments (the Law).

In Deuteronomy 11:18-21 the Israelites are told how they are to follow the Law (God's laws):
1. Fix/instill them in their hearts and minds
2. Wear them as symbols
3. Teach them to their children

4. Talk about them at all times—at home, as they travel, morning and night.

5. Display the teachings in their home

Questions for consideration:

1. Is this a new day requiring new laws, or is there a need to return to the "basics"?

2. How has our teaching or lack of teaching contributed to the breakdown of families?

   a. Do we teach our children right from wrong? Do they have a conscience? Do they have faith? hope?

   b. Look at the messages on tee shirts; do they convey Christian values?

   c. Children learn primarily through repetition; adults most often learn when the experience demands it. Does your whole demeanor and attitude teach what you believe?

   d. What is taught in your home? on posters or artwork? on television—MTV, cable? in magazines? through music and other media?

   e. Are you willing to say as Joshua in Joshua 24:15, "Choose this day whom you will serve. . . but as for me and my household, we will serve the LORD"?

Outline #3

Titles:
   1. Stones of Promise
   2. How We Got Over

Scripture: Joshua 4:4-7; Joshua 4:21-24

Background: Joshua tells each of the twelve tribes to appoint a man to carry a stone to be placed as a memorial to the people of Israel. The stones are set up in Gilgal as a memorial so that future generations will remember what God did for the people who crossed the Jordan and the

Red Sea. We are always to remember that God is powerful and that we should love the Lord.

This sermon calls the people to faith and hope, remembering how God has been with them at the most difficult times.

Situations for remembering (memorializing):

1. Birth and survival of a seriously at-risk child

2. Recovery of a person whom doctors have given up on

3. Survival in disasters (earthquake, fire, flood, hurricane, tornados)

4. Successful efforts to reclaim community

5. Renewal of marriage vows

6. Church anniversaries, reunions, homecomings

7. Growth through loss and grieving

8. Moments in black history

9. Struggles and accomplishments in the church

10. Celebration of families.

Survey of Congregational Ministries with Families

Approaches to Serving Families:

Describe programs in which your congregation serves families:

Describe major ways in which the pastor(s) serve(s) families:

Describe ways (if any) in which the congregation joins with other church groups to serve families:

Describe ways (if any) in which your congregation works with community groups in supporting/serving families:

What are the major problems facing families seeking help in your congregation?

Survey of Family Needs and Interests

1. Tell us about your family:

A. Family composition:

single young adult
young couple, no children
single-parent family with children
two-parent family with children
older parent(s) with grown children
older parent(s) with adult children at home
single-member family, widowed or divorced
single-member family never married
blended family with children at home
other (specify)

B. Number of children living at home:
Ages

2. Tell us about your concerns:

A. Check those issues that are of greatest concern for your family and the families in the community:

child-care needs   racism
alcoholism   aging parents
drug abuse   crime
stress   disrespect of elderly
unemployment   child abuse
step-parenting   single parenting
inadequate schools   helping children in school
teen pregnancy   teen suicide
divorce   gangs
other _____   other _____

B. What do you think all families need?

Check five (prioritize by placing a 1 next to the greatest need/concern, a 2 next to the next greatest one, and so forth until five are ranked).

_____ more time together   _____ simpler lifestyle

_____ counseling services   _____ good child care

_____ tutoring   _____ better schools

_____ training in parenting skills   _____ intergenerational activities

_____ approval/support from others   _____ communication skills

_____ help in resolving conflicts   _____ workshops on Christian sexual behavior

_____ family worship experiences   _____ increased participation in the church

_____ greater influence with their children   _____ interpersonal relationship skills

_____ knowledge about teaching Christian   _____ opportunities for spiritual growth at home
        values in the home   and at church

_____ more recreation or social opportunities
        with other families

_____ community resources used more
        effectively

_____ ways to work together as a family to
        help others

_____ opportunities for spiritual growth at home and at church

C. Programs/activities you would like to see the church offer to families:

D. Other things you would like to share with us?

Opinion Survey

Do you view any of the following as problems in your community? Please check one response for each item.

	No problem	**A problem**	**A big problem**
1. Poverty			
2. Unemployment			
3. Alcohol use			
4. Drug use			
5. High crime rate			
6. Conflict within families			
7. Domestic violence			
8. Child abuse			
9. Unplanned pregnancies			
10. Lack of sex education			
11. Racial/ethnic prejudice			
12. Religious conflicts			
13. People moving in or out of the area			
14. Physical distance between neighbors			
15. Lack of neighborliness			
16. Lack of recreational opportunities			
17. Lack of services for senior citizens			
18. Inadequate transportation			
19. Environment neglect			
20. Lack of housing for physically/mentally challenged people			
21. Lack of employment options for physically/mentally challenged people			
22. Unresponsive social agencies			
23. Knowledge of where to get help			
24. Illiteracy			
25. Crowded jails or prisons			
26. Lack of child-care facilities			
27. Marriage/family breakdown			

Are there other problems not listed above?

Of all those items you marked as "A problem" or "A big problem," which are the top two?

What would you like to see done about them?

Sources for Information Gathering

1. United States Bureau of Census
2. Federal and state clearinghouses for information and statistics
3. Bureau of Labor Statistics reports
4. Vital and Health Statistics Series
5. Federal, state, county, and city departments of health and human services, labor, education, and so forth.
6. Federations of social and/or health organizations
7. Local and regional planning councils
8. City, county, and regional planning departments
9. City or county health and welfare departments
10. Local or national organizations in a specific field
11. Local schools
12. Law enforcement and judicial departments
13. Chambers of commerce
14. Colleges and universities
15. Research organizations
16. United Way
17. Television and radio stations
18. National or local trade associations
19. Public library

Denominational Resources

African Methodist Episcopal Church

AME Journal of Christian Education features articles on family ministries. The subscription price is $15.00 a year. *Handbook for Christian Education* by Kenneth H. Hill, Ph.D., Executive Secretary of Christian Education Department of the AME Church, $10.00.

To order, send payment to AME Church, Christian Education Department, 500 8th Avenue South, Nashville, TN 37203.

African Methodist Episcopal Zion Church

CHRISTKWANZA, an Afro-American church liturgy, by Dr. Ndugu T' Ofori-Atta, and *The Curriculum Guide for Children* can be ordered from the Department of Christian Education, Inc., African Methodist Episcopal Church, Zion, P.O. Box 32305, Charlotte, NC 28232-2305.

American Baptist Churches

A packet on prevention of child abuse. For more information, contact the Director of Black Church Education and Children's Ministries, Educational Ministries, American Baptist Churches, (215) 768-2149.

A packet on family violence. For more information, contact the Director of Family Ministries, National Ministries, American Baptist Churches at (215)768-2154.

The Christian Church (Disciples of Christ)

The Church in the Life of the Black Family: A Study Guide by Louise Bates Evans, a resource to be used with Wallace Charles Smith's book *The Church in the Life of the Black Family.* This resource is part of Stepping Stones for Christian Growth, an elective curriculum series. To order or for more information, call Christian Board of Publications at (800) 366-3383.

A Child Protection Packet, which includes a catalogue from the National Committee to Prevent Child Abuse and child protection information for congregations; *Family Matters,* a free quarterly newsletter dealing with family issues; *For the Children,* a free bimonthly newsletter about children's issues. All resources are available from Reverend Jane Lawrence at Homeland

Ministries, P.O. Box 1986, Indianapolis, IN 46206, (317) 635-3100, extension 340.

Evangelical Lutheran Church of America

Family Resources Series, four-page leaflets dealing with a variety of critical issues in family living. Order from The Division for Church in Society—Deptartment for Education and Program Resources, 8765 W. Higgins Road, Chicago, IL 60631, (312) 380-2687.

National Baptist Convention, USA, Inc.

Healing for the Broken Family Circle, A Manual for Family Ministry, by Enoch L. Jones, $9.95; a study guide to complement the manual by Alvin C. Bernstine, $10.00. To order, send payment to Sunday School Publishing Board, 330 Charlotte Pike, Nashville, TN 37218, or call (615) 256-2480.

Presbyterian Church (U.S.A.)

Family Violence, A Study and Action Guide for Congregations, edited by Patricia Gill Turner, a staff associate for Justice for Women. This guide is a continued effort to break the silence in the church about family violence. For more information, call (502) 569-5636.

United Methodist Church

Families Matter, a complete resource guide to planning family ministry, by Marilyn Magee, $5.00. *Stones of Promise*, a video addressing African American Family life. Both resources can be ordered through Cokesbury Bookstore (615) 749-6123 or the United Methodist Publishing House (615) 749-6113.

Social Service Agencies:

Balm of Gilead

Center for Prevention of Sexual and Domestic Violence

Children's Defense Fund

National Association for the Advancement of Colored People (NAACP)

National Black Child Development Institute

National Congress of Black Churches

Urban League

Program/Project Action Plan

Goal

Objectives

Tasks/Activities   **Whose responsibility?**   **By when?**

Resources

Evaluation

Did you accomplish the objectives? How successful were you?

Where do we go from here? What is needed?

Program/Project Action Plan: Timeline

Beginning Date:

Initiating steps:
1.
2.
3.
4.
5.

Three months:
1.
2.
3.
4.
5.

Review needed? Reassignments?

Six months:
1.
2.
3.
4.
5.

Progress report needed?

Nine months:
1.
2.
3.
4.
5.

Review needed? Sailing smoothly?

Twelve months:
1.
2.
3.
4.
5.

Program/Project Action Plan

Resource Assessment Data

Community Institutions/Organizations

Name	Address	Telephone
1.		
2.		
3.		

Resource Persons (in the congregation, community)

Name	Address	Telephone
1.		
2.		
3.		

Financial Resources

Church Budget: $ _____

   Missions $ _____

   Outreach and Nurture $ _____

   Education $ _____

   Age-Level and Family Ministries $ _____

   Special Funds $ _____

   Other, Individual Contributions $ _____

   Fundraising Activities $ _____

Other Sources: _____

     $ _____

     $ _____

     $ _____

Additional Services/Resources

Family Ministry Models and Consultants

Models of Family Ministries for the Black Church

The following five models of family ministry programs were a part of the Black Family Ministry Project. The consultants, in training, made visits to several of these sites during the course of this project.

The Fathers' Center

4601 State Street, Room 320
East St. Louis, IL 62205

The Fathers' Center is a program designed to help black males overcome poverty, unemployment, and other societal stresses that destroy family life. The Fathers' Center is a program of Lutheran Child and Family Services of Illinois (LCFS), a statewide social service agency assisting children and families since 1873. The Center's staff provide counseling (marital counseling is an essential component of the program), vocational assistance, and emergency assistance to meet basic physical needs.

The Fathers' Center is a respected and renowned ministry that has a proven track record with high praise from the participants. Those who have benefited from the Fathers' Center program say:

"When I need to talk to someone, I come to the Center instead of taking my pain to the streets."

— Leonard

"It's all about being somebody. Due to the confidence they gave me, I was able to start a painting business."

— Everett

"We need to go out and make money, but first we need the basics. If you have that one leg to stand on, you have a better chance."

— Tommie

Brick By Brick Family Ministries

Citizen of Zion Missionary Baptist Church
12930 N. Lime Avenue
Compton, CA 90221

Brick By Brick Family Ministries is a program designed and structured to guide and aid families in the church. The purpose of

Brick By Brick is to build family bonds through spiritual awareness, specifically by getting back to the Word of God.

Brick By Brick Family Ministries recognizes that the family structure, God's institutional plan for the family, is being ripped apart by satanic devices and needs to be put back on the right track.

The Primary Goal

The main goal is to help families and churches build ministries that will revitalize the once productive and vital community in order to renew its sense of character and other life-giving attributes.

Through a seven-phase plan, Brick By Brick aids every level of the church family:

Phase 1: Heart to Heart Ministry aids young people ages 13-18 in developing positive decision-making skills.

Phase 2: Bridges (Teen Pregnancy Ministry) is geared to affirm and support young women before and after pregnancy.

Phase 3: The Miracle Workers (Ministry to Married Couples) is aimed at giving support both to healthy couples and to those who are struggling.

Phase 4: Budgeting Our Finances (Financial Planning) is a ministry geared toward assisting with home financial management.

Phase 5: Enrichment House Program provides couples in the church with the opportunity to live in a three-bedroom home rent free, while paying off all debts and saving to purchase their own home.

Phase 6: The Crisis Program aims to introduce young men ages 18-22 to manhood through developing decision-making, discipleship, and destiny-planning skills.

Phase 7: The Crisis Program aims to introduce young women ages 17-22 to adulthood through developing decision-making, discipleship, and destiny-planning skills.

Each phase of the ministry symbolizes a victorious step in Christ Jesus!

The Organizational Chart for Brick By Brick Family Ministries

Coordinator of Family-Life Ministries
Project Director
Single Adult Ministries
Program Leader for Never Marrieds
Program Leader for Former Marrieds
Program Leader for Widowed Singles
Program Leader for Churchwide Singles' Events

Project Director
Married Couples Ministry
Program Leader for Couples without Children
Program Leader for Couples with Preschool Children
Program Leader for Couples with Young Children
Program Leader for Couples with Teenagers
Program Leader for Couples with Grown Children

Project Director
Parents and Children's Intergenerational Ministry
Program Leader for Bible Study Activities
Program Leader for Arts and Crafts
Program Leader for Missions/Outreach
Program Leader for Special Interest

Project Director
Senior Adults Ministry
Program Leader for Senior Adults Still Active in the Church
Program Leader for Institutionalized Senior Adults
Program Leader for Homebound Senior Adults
Program Leader for Special Projects of Senior Adults

SISTERS

A.P. Shaw United Methodist Church
2525 12th Place, S.E.
Washington, DC 20020

SISTERS is a teen pregnancy prevention and intervention project. The intent of SISTERS is to help teen mothers come to terms with the reality of their pregnancy and support them as they prepare for the coming of a new life. The project provides evaluation of the teen mother's medical and emotional condition at the time of her initial interview phase. A comprehensive evaluation form on each mother is followed by referrals and assistance when needed.

SISTERS is also a teen mothers support group, offering understanding, support, and encouragement during the nine months of pregnancy and follow-up evaluations for three years after the birth.

SISTERS program services include:

1. Comprehensive evaluation and health-care maintenance program
2. Support group
3. Parenting classes
4. Baby showers
5. Delivery room support
6. Educational encouragement
7. Field trips
8. Teen pregnancy prevention program
9. Father's Day Apart

The women of A.P. Shaw continue the covenant of Ruth as outlined in the Old Testament Scripture by advocating for physical, mental, and spiritual wholeness:

> Entreat me not to leave you or to return from following you; for where you go I will go, and where you lodge I will lodge; your people shall be my people, and your God my God (Ruth 1:16, RSV).

The GodFathers Program

Progressive Baptist Church
1419 12th Avenue South
Nashville, TN 37212

Recruiting responsible African American men, mainly police officers and church leaders, to serve as mentors to African American male youth, the GodFathers Program formally pledges a commitment to young black males.

The GodFathers Program is a serious attempt to address the critical crisis in many black communities, that is, the economic, political, social, and educational victimization of black males, coupled with the absence of black male parental figures in many homes.

Through intentional efforts: educational, supporting, and parent groups, the GodFathers program works to cooperate, collaborate, and integrate its activities with existing programs such as the Nashville-based Men of Distinction, Boy Scouts, Little League, and tutorial programs.

Participants are involved in such activities as:

- adult male\child rap sessions
- PTA and other formal educational development
- church attendance
- skills and conflict management
- development of respect for women
- substance abuse-free lifestyles
- financial management
- library skills development.

The GodFathers Program challenges and supports young males as they foster the lifestyle and skills to overcome the obstacles and barriers that threaten to destroy them.

Shiloh Family Life Center

Shiloh Baptist Church
1510 Ninth Street, N.W.
Washington, DC 20001

A Special Place for Spiritual, Mental and Physical Development

The Shiloh Family Life Center is a facility in the nation's capital, which is as unique as it is versatile. Located just six blocks from the D.C. Convention Center, the Shiloh Family Life Center houses a comprehensive program of activities that provide educational and cultural awareness, spiritual renewal, and recreational relaxation and that contribute to personal and group development.

Program activities include:

- weddings
- luncheons and forums
- seminars and workshops
- sports clinics and tournaments
- graduation receptions
- bridal and baby showers

Shiloh's branch of the Boy's and Girl's Club

The center includes five spacious floors containing the Heritage Banquet Hall; the Roof Garden Terrace; the Chapel of Hope; the Tuning Fork (restaurant); game rooms; an arts and crafts room; a specialty shop; and a fully equipped health, fitness, and athletic club with weight room, indoor jogging track, full-size sauna, racquetball courts, eight-person Jacuzzi, and a regulation-size basketball court.

All program activities are provided in a serene environment linking God and community and fostering togetherness.

Black Family Ministry Consultants

African Methodist Episcopal Church

Jacquelyn Bullock	Brooklyn, NY
Strelsa Jeffries	Baltimore, MD
Rev. E. Holmes Matthews	Memphis, TN
Dr. Leslie Skinner	Philadelphia, PA

African Methodist Episcopal Zion Church

Rev. Reginald Carter	Tuscaloosa, AL
Vertel Govan	Brooklyn, NY
Evelyn F. Holden	Park Forest, IL
Rev. Raymon Hunt	Charlotte, NC
Rev. Douglas Maven	Patterson, NJ
Martina Parker-Sobers	Lauderhill, FL
Theodore E. Shaw	Chicago, IL
Darryle B. Starnes	New Britain, CT
Rev. Roy Swann	Los Angeles, CA
Dr. Ndugu Gb T'Ofori-Atta	Atlanta, GA

American Baptist Churches

Rev. Duane Brown	Cleveland, OH
Rev. Alfloyd Butler	Chicago, IL
Yvonne Carter	Cleveland, OH
Rev. Dwight Cook	Rochester, NY
Rev. Dr. Ronald English	Charleston, WV
Rev. William Hairston	Boston, MA
Rev. Edward Harper	Newark, NJ
Rev. Ella M. Ivey	Bronx, NY
Rev. Dr. John T. Leftwich	Murrayville, PA
Marcella Leftwich	New York
Jonnie Lewis-Thorpe	New Haven, CT
Rev. M. Frances Manning	New Jersey
Dr. Mamie O. Oliver	Providence, RI
Rev. Robert L. Stephens	Kansas City, MO
Rev. Dozell Varner	Sterling, IL
Rev. Mylion Waite	University Heights, OH
Barbara Waller	Downers Grove, IL

Christian Church (Disciples)

Michele R. Brown	Indianapolis, IN
Betty Miller Green	Chicago, IL
Rev. Robin E. Hedgeman	Elyria, OH
Ruby F. Henry	Dallas, TX
Rev. Cathryn Teer Hodge	Indianapolis, IN
Rev. Timothy L. James	Cleveland, OH

| Rev. Laurice A. Valentine | Kansas City, MO |
| Rev. J.O. Williams, Sr. | Wilson, NC |

Christian Methodist Episcopal Church

Bennie Barnes	Richmond, CA
Barbara C. Campbell	Stone Mountain, GA
Bryan L. Champion	Washington, DC
Laquita Cole	Richmond, CA
Rev. Katheryn Hazel	Hartwell, GA
Rev. Chester Tollette	Richmond, CA
Gloria White	Jackson, MS
Rev. Sylvester Williams	Birmingham, AL

Evangelical Lutheran Church in America

Trevor Bolden	Lithonia, GA
Mattie Crumpton	Fort Worth, TX
Michelle Ellison	Wuandanch, NY
Betty Esters	Detroit, MI
Rev. Cedric Gibb	Orangeburg, SC
Deborah Hazel	Philadelphia, PA
Linda J. Holmes	Roosevelt, NY
Patricia Johnson	Detroit, MI
Lorraine Lett	Bronx, NY
Harolyn C. Light	St. Louis, MO
Mary Loper	Jackson, MS
Darlene Love	Hawthorne, CA
Rev. James Phillips	Chicago, IL
Helena Prophete	St. Louis, MO
Beverly Silveri	Atlanta, GA
Grace Vedder	Washington, DC
Charlotte Williams	Chicago, IL
Lela Williams	Chicago, IL
Maxine Young	Philadelphia, PA
Synovia Hardy Youngblood	Fullerton, CA

The Moravian Church in America

| Blondell Jones | Bronx, NY |

National Baptist Convention, USA, Inc.

Dr. Elaine Baker	Albany, GA
Rev. Alvin Bernstine	Brooklyn, NY
Rev. Karen Jones Bernstine	Brooklyn, NY
Rev. Raymond Bowman	Nashville, TN
Rev. Gregory Jackson	Hackensack, NJ
Rev. Loretta Veney	Philadelphia, PA
Rev. Michael Starks	Compton, CA

Presbyterian Church (U.S.A.)

Patricia Berry	San Diego, CA
Ella Busby	Columbus, GA
Cheri Chappelle	Chicago, IL
Rev. Sandra Edwards	Detroit, MI
Rev. Arlene Gordon	Hercules, CA
Rev. Kevin R. Johnson	Detroit, MI
Terry S. Johnson	Brooklyn, NY
Linda P. Marks Thomas	Charlotte, NC
Sandra Martin	Charlotte, NC
Mildred McGee	Bronx, NY
Geraldine Murdock	Atlanta, GA
Rev. Mary Neuben-Williams	Holland, MI
Brenda Oliver	East Point, GA
Denice Praileau-Franklin	Los Angeles, CA
Stanley Stephens	Oak Park, IL
Ethelyn Taylor	Philadelphia, PA
Diane Wright	Sumter, SC

United Church of Christ

| Sammie Dortch | Chicago, IL |

United Methodist Church

Amanda Edmondson	Nashville, TN
Joyce Favors	Evanston, IL
Vivian Fielder	Nashville, TN
Alma Fields	Chicago, IL
Barbara Ann Hawes	Bloomfield, MI

The consultants may be contacted through the staff person of each denomination listed in this appendix.

The Role of the Consultant

In a highly complex world where no one person can know everything, many churches are looking to resource persons with specific expertise. Such resource persons are usually consultants. Consultants are often utilized to assist in sharpening insights, developing new skills, and enhancing a program/ministry that is already in place.

The Family Ministry Consultant is trained to assist congregations in initiating and/or strengthening ministry with families in the congregation and community.

The Family Ministry Consultant is:

1. *A helper* who promotes family ministry and encourages the congregation in its efforts.

2. *A catalyst* who raises the awareness of the pastor and the congregation.

3. *A motivator* who presents information that stimulates the congregation's concern for families.

4. *An enabler* who helps the congregation gather data and identify needs.

5. *A diagnostician* who assists in analyzing gathered data and helping the congregation explore alternatives.

6. *An advisor/technician* who is available during the planning stages of the ministry.

7. *A resource person* who assists the committee/congregation in networking with other congregations and agencies and identifying resources and people.

8. *A visionary* who advocates for families and for ministry to/with families.

9. *A facilitator* who stands by the ministry from conceptualization through implementation and evaluation.

What a Consultant Is — and Is Not

The consultant is:

an educator—not the group leader.
a trainer—not an operator.
an advisor—not a policy setter.
a counselor—not a manipulator.
a technician—not an administrator.
an influencer—not a dominator.
a helper—not a director.

Overall, a Family Ministry Consultant is one who assists the congregation in hearing God's call to minister to families in the church and community, then steps back and observes the church answer that call. Each congregation and community is unique, and its ministry will reflect that uniqueness with the assistance of a consultant.

National Staff Team

Josselyn Bennett

Evangelical Lutheran Church of America
8765 W. Higgins Road
Chicago, IL 60631
(312) 380-2687

Josselyn Bennett was born in Mobile, Alabama. She moved to Columbus, Ohio, after high school to attend Capital University. Mrs. Bennett graduated from Capital University with a major in social work and received a masters in social work from Ohio State University. She worked as a social worker for five years and as Executive Director of Project Linden Counseling Center for ten years. During her tenure with Project Linden, Mrs. Bennett developed programs to meet the needs of women and youth.

Currently, Mrs. Bennett is Director for Age-Span Ministries in the Division for Church in Society of the Evangelical Lutheran Church in America, located in Chicago.

Mrs. Bennett has served on numerous boards, has been active in various Lutheran congregations, and has received many honors and awards for community service. She attends Bethel Lutheran Church in Chicago.

Alvin C. Bernstine

National Baptist Convention, U.S.A., Inc.
Department of Family Ministry
Sunday School Publishing Board
230 Decatur Street
Brooklyn, NY 11233
(718) 493-8770

Rev. Alvin C. Bernstine is a native of Oakland, California. He is a third-generation Baptist preacher, as well as the brother of a preacher. His wife, Karen, is also a Baptist preacher. He received his primary education in the public schools of Oakland; a bachelor of arts (*magna cum laude*) from Bishop College, Dallas, Texas; a master of divinity from Vanderbilt Divinity School, Nashville, Tennessee, and a doctor of ministry from United Theological Seminary, Dayton, Ohio.

Rev. Bernstine is currently serving as pastor of the Mount Lebanon Baptist Church, Brooklyn, New York, and is Director of Family Ministry Programs of the Sunday School Publishing Board, National Baptist Convention, U.S.A. Rev. Bernstine's work brings him into direct contact with nearly eight million National Baptists. In addition to many articles for *The Informer, A Journal of Christian Education*, he has written several books: *How to Organize a Department of Christian Education in the Local Church*: *A Congregational Enablement Model*; *As For Me and My House*, a book of sermons on the Black family; and *Healing the Broken Family Circle*, a study guide to complement the book of the same title.

George L. Blackwell (Retired)

General Secretary Christian Education
African Methodist Episcopal Zion Church
Chicago, IL

Ronald Cunningham

Christian Methodist Episcopal Church
Elvis Presley Blvd., Suite 214
Memphis, TN 38116
(901) 345-0580

Dr. Ronald M. Cunningham has served as General Secretary of the Department of Christian Education of the Christian Methodist Episcopal Church since his election by the denomination's 1986 General Conference. In this capacity he also served as editor of Church School Resources and Director of Higher Education. A former college professor and vice-president, he has been a minister and educator for more than twenty-eight years. A youth minister, a professor of religion and philosophy at Lane College, Jackson, Tennessee, and vice-president of Miles College, Birmingham, Alabama, Dr. Cunningham has also served as West Coast Regional Director of Operation PUSH (1976). He has been a community center director and a social service caseworker, and has served as pastor in churches in California, Tennessee, and Alabama.

A native of Chicago, Illinois, Dr. Cunningham graduated from Charles Summer High School in St. Louis. He spent three years in the United States Marine Corps where he served as an administrative aide. He received a bachelor of arts in social science from LeMoyne College, Memphis, Tennessee, and a doctor of religion from the School of Theology at Claremont, California. He is a member of Omega Psi Phi Fraternity, Inc.

L. Rita Dixon

Presbyterian Church (U.S.A.)
100 Witherspoon St., Rm. 2B2006
Louisville, KY 40202
(502) 569-5697

Dr. L. Rita Dixon is an ordained Presbyterian clergywoman serving in the national office of the Presbyterian Church USA's Racial Ethnic Ministry Unit. Her role as Coordinator of Black Congregational Enhancement is broad and diverse. A major focus is working with staff, lay leaders, and clergy across the denomination to provide programs that nurture spirituality, faith development, community ministries, and effective use of Presbyterian policy in black congregations.

Before becoming a clergyperson, Dr. Dixon was an educator, teaching high school mathematics for nine years and college mathematics for two years. After completing a doctorate in curriculum and supervision, she was a curriculum developer and teacher for six years. Her special interest is in the areas of religion and psychology, African and African American religious traditions, and biblical studies. Her strongest skills are in program and leader development. She is presently working on program development for congregations in the following areas: single adult ministries; a comprehensive approach to Bible study; spiritual growth groups using a Christian version of the Twelve Step process; evangelism; community ministries; and teenage enrichment programs.

Jerome B. Dorsey

5024 South Elkhart Court
Aurora, CO 80015
(303) 693-9404 (home)
(303) 427-7553 (office)

Rev. Jerome B. Dorsey is the Assistant to the Bishop of the Rocky Mountain Synod of the Evangelical Lutheran Church in America. He is responsible for planning, administering, and coordinating the Synod's Congregational Ministries program activities including worship, witness, evangelism, education, outdoor ministries, family life, congregational planning, youth, stewardship, leadership training, and related congregational programs.

Rev. Dorsey also serves as consultant for African American Ministries in the Evangelical Lutheran Church in America's (ELCA) Commission for Multicultural Ministries (CMM) which provides services, advice, and counsel to assist the ECLA in working toward the goal of full partnership and participation of African Americans, Asians, Hispanics, and Native Americans in the life of the church and society. The former director of its African American Ministries program, Rev. Dorsey is specifically responsible for providing consultative services, advice, and counsel in the development of policies, programs, and other means to enable the ECLA to meet its goal of full partnership with African Americans and the African American community.

Louise Bates Evans

1502 W. 26th Street
Indianapolis, IN 46208
(317) 926-8413

Dr. Louise Bates Evans, Project Director, retired from the general staff of the Christian

Church (Disciples of Christ) where she was Director of Family and Children's Ministries for the Division of Homeland Ministries, with offices in Indianapolis, Indiana. She served in this position for eleven years, developing programs and training regional and local church leaders.

Prior to joining the staff of the Christian Church, Dr. Evans was Assistant Professor in Family Studies at Virginia Polytechnic Institute and State University at Blacksburg, Virginia, and Purdue University in West Lafayette, Indiana. She has also served as Visiting Professor at Winthrop College, Rock Hill, South Carolina, and Indiana University/Purdue University, School of Social Services in Indianapolis, Indiana.

In retirement, Dr. Evans continues her commitment to Christian education and the family. She is currently teaching Issues in Christian Education: Ministry with Children and Family Ministry at Christian Theological Seminary, the Disciples of Christ Seminary in Indianapolis. She says that her work and concern for the church's response to families spans more than twenty-five years, and she is still on the journey and no ways tired.

Kenneth Hill

African Methodist Episcopal Church
500 8th Avenue, South
Nashville, TN 37203
(615) 242-1420

Dr. Kenneth H. Hill is an experienced Christian educator, professor, teacher, and pastor. Dr. Hill serves as Executive Secretary of Christian Education, African Methodist Episcopal Church. As adjunct faculty member at Vanderbilt Divinity School, Dr. Hill is currently teaching The African American Church Ministry to Black Families.

Dr. Hill has a bachelors degree from Wayne State University, a masters in theological studies from Harvard Divinity School, and an M.A. and Ph.D. from the University of Michigan. Dr. Hill says his current involvement in family ministry is a further step in his spiritual journey in ministry.

Raymon E. Hunt

African Methodist Episcopal Zion Church
P.O. Box 32305
Charlotte, NC 28232-2305
(704) 332-9323

Rev. Raymon E. Hunt is an ordained African Methodist Episcopal Church, Zion (A.M.E.Z.) pastor who has served in many capacities with the A.M.E.Z. Church. Currently serving as Secretary/Treasurer of the Christian Education Department of the A.M.E.Z. Church, Rev. Hunt was also trained as a consultant in the Black Family Ministry Project.

As an author, Rev. Hunt published an anthology on prayer. He is married and has two daughters.

Edgar L. Mack, Team Chair (Deceased)

General Secretary Christian Education
African Methodist Episcopal Church
Nashville, TN

Marilyn Ruth Williams Magee

United Methodist Church
P.O. Box 840
Nashville, TN 37202
(615) 340-7597

Ms. Marilyn Williams Magee was born and reared in southern Illinois. Her life was shaped in large measure by the strong faith of her parents, one Methodist, one Baptist. Choosing to claim her Methodist heritage, Marilyn is a fourth generation member of the United Methodist denomination.

Educated in Illinois, Marilyn has achieved the following distinctions: valedictorian in high school; bachelor of science with double majors in elementary and special education; master of science in education specializing in supervision and administration; postgraduate studies. She is a Danforth Foundation Scholar and was cited for reading research by the John F. Kennedy Center of Peabody University.

Ms. Magee's work experience includes: caseworker for public assistance; cancer detection and research; teacher, counselor, and administrator for Chicago Public Schools; Executive Director of Chicago Black Methodists for Church Renewal; and member of the General Board of Discipleship of the United Methodist Church. She is currently developing two program emphases on Family and Conference relations. She is also a staff trainer for Quality Improvement Management Systems, conducting staff and conference training.

As an active participant in religious and educational pursuits, Ms. Magee is a believer in connecting faith and works. She conducts spiritual retreats and actively promotes the concept of sisterhood. Her personal statement: "I am a Christian under construction endeavoring to effectively utilize the gifts loaned to me by God while on this earthly sojourn."

Virginia Sargent (Retired)

615 Hazlewood Ave.
Ardmore, PA 19003
(610) 649-9844

Dr. Virginia (Ginger) Sargent is a native of Brooklyn, New York. She was baptized into church membership before her seventh birthday. She responded to a call to professional church leadership by studying at Hart-ford Seminary, where she received an M.A., and Eastern Baptist Theological Seminary, where she completed a doctor of ministry degree. Her thesis includes a workshop for local churches entitled "Celebrating the Strengths of Black Families."

Dr. Sargent has been an editor of church school materials, a workshop leader teaching in the church school, and author of numerous articles. She was formerly Director of Black Church Education in the Department of Education for Discipleship, American Baptist Churches in the U.S.A.

Jack Sullivan, Jr.

The Christian Church (Disciples of Christ)
P.O. Box 1986
Indianapolis, IN 46206
(317) 353-1499, Ext. 345

Rev. Dr. Jack Sullivan, Jr. is an ordained minister with the Christian Church (Disciples of Christ), USA and Canada. He serves the Disciples' Division of Homeland Ministries as Associate for Racial/Ethnic and Multicultural Educational Ministries. Through this office, he develops resources and programs relevant to African American and Hispanic American Disciples, while working to create multicultural approaches to educational ministry.

As a resident of Indianapolis, Indiana, Rev. Sullivan volunteers with Big Brothers and the American Heart Association.

Rev. Sullivan's understanding of ministry has been shaped by his study of black liberation theology. "I believe that all congregations are called by God to become engaged in ministries which meet the immediate needs of people as well as to work for the systematic change which can break the chains of racial injustice, poverty, and crime. With our traditional understanding and experience of Jesus Christ to be Liberator, the African American church (youth, adults, laity, and clergy) must now become equipped to work for Christ's liberation and wholeness in African American families and communities."

Sponsoring Agency of
The Black Family Ministry Project

Ministries in Christian Education
National Council of Churches of Christ
475 Riverside Drive, Room 708
New York, NY 10115

Bibliography

Books

Billingsley, Andrew. *Black Families and the Struggle for Survival*. New York: Friendship Press, 1974.

Billingsley, Andrew. *Climbing Jacob's Ladder*. New York: Simon & Schuster, 1992.

Daley, Shannon and Kathleen Guy. *Welcome the Child: A Child Advocacy Guide for Churches.* New York: Children's Defense Fund and Friendship Press, 1994.

Edelman, Marian Wright. *Families in Peril: An Agenda for Social Change*. Cambridge, Mass.: Harvard University Press, 1987.

Felder, Cain Hope. *Troubling Biblical Waters: Race, Class, and Family.* Maryknoll, N.Y.: Orbis Books, 1989.

Friedman, Edwin H. *Generation to Generation: Family Process in Church and Synagogue*. New York: The Guilford Press, 1985.

Hare, Nathan and Julia Hare. *The Endangered Black Family*. San Francisco: Black Think Tank, 1984.

Hauk, Gary H. *Family Enrichment in Your Church*. Nashville: Convention Press, 1988.

Hearne, Kathryn, ed. *A Tennesseans Guide to Grassroots Advocacy*. Nashville: Tennessee Hunger Coalition, 1989.

Hill, Robert B. *The Strength of Black Families*. National Urban League.

Howell, John C. *Church and Family Growing Together*. Nashville: Broadman Press, 1984.

Lewis, Jerry M. and John G. Looney. *The Long Struggle: Well-Functioning Working Class Black Families*. New York: Brunner/Mazel, 1983.

McClain, William B. *Traveling Light*. New York: Friendship Press, 1981.

Rickerson, Wayne E. *How to Help the Christian Home, Your Church Can Minister to Families*. Ventura, Calif.: Regal Books, 1978.

Roberts, J. Deotis. *Roots of a Black Future: Family and Church*, Philadelphia: Westminster Press, 1980.

Some', Malidoma Patrice. *Rituals*. Portland, Ore.: Swan Raven & Company, 1993.

Smith, Wallace Charles. *The Church in the Life of the Black Family*. Valley Forge, Pa.: Judson Press, 1985.

Video

The Biblical Basis for Family Ministry. Leadership Training Project for Family Ministry in Black Congregations, Phase I, Training

Session 2. Chevy Chase, Maryland, 1991.

A Partial List of Suggested Readings

Bell-Scott, Patricia. *Double Stitch: Black Women Write About Mothers and Daughters*. Boston: Beacon Press, 1991.

Benson, Janice Hale. *Black Children, Their Roots and Culture*. Baltimore: Johns Hopkins University, 1986.

Bernstine, Alvin C. *As For Me and My House: Some Redemptive Words for the Black Family*. Nashville: Townsend Press, 1993.

Bolton, Frank G., Jr. *The Pregnant Adolescent: Problems of Premature Parenthood*. Beverly Hills: Sage, 1980.

Dobbins, Richard D. *The Family-Friendly Church, A Caring Church in a Broken World*. Altamonte Springs, Fla.: Creation House, 1989.

Edleman, Marian Wright. *The Measure of Our Success: A Letter to My Children and Yours*. Boston: Beacon Press, 1992.

Foster, Charles R. and Shockley, Grant S. *Working with Black Youth: Opportunities for Christian Ministry*. Nashville: Abingdon Press, 1989.

Karenga, Maulana. *Kwanzaa: Origin, Concepts, Practice*. Los Angeles: Kwaida Publications, 1977.

Kunjufu, Jawanza. *Countering the Conspiracy to Destroy Our Black Boys* (two volumes). Chicago: African American Images, 1985.

Kunjufu, Jawanza. *Developing Positive Self-Images and Disciplines in Black Children*. Chicago: African American Images, 1984.

Madhubuti, Haki. *Black Men: Obsolete, Single, and Dangerous*. Chicago: Third World Press, 1990.

McCray, Walter A. *Reaching and Teaching Black Young Adults*. Chicago: Black Light Fellowship Publications, 1986.

Staples, Robert. *The World of Black Singles: Changing Patterns of Male-Female Relations*. Westport, Conn.: Greenwood Press, 1981.

Wangerin, Walter Jr. *As For Me and My House: Crafting Your Marriage to Last*. Nashville: Thomas Nelson Publishers, 1990.

Weems, Renita J. *Just a Sister Away: A Womanist Vision of Women's Relationships in the Bible*. San Diego, Calif.: LuraMedia Publishers, 1988.